# Culturally Sustaining Pedagogies in Music Education

This volume problematizes the historic dominance of Western classical music education and posits culturally sustaining pedagogy (CSP) as a framework through which music curricula can better serve increasingly diverse student populations.

By detailing a qualitative study conducted in an urban high school in the United States, the volume illustrates how traditional approaches to music education can inhibit student engagement and learning. Moving beyond culturally responsive teaching, the volume goes on to demonstrate how enhancing teachers' understanding of alternative musical epistemologies can support them in embracing CSP in the music classroom. This new theoretical and pedagogical framework reconceptualizes current practices to better sustain the musical cultures of the minoritized.

This text will benefit researchers, academics, and educators with an interest in music education, multicultural education, and urban education more broadly. Those specifically interested in ethnomusicology and classroom practice will also benefit from this book.

**Emily Good-Perkins** is an Instructor of Voice, Vocal Pedagogy, and the History and Philosophy of Music Education. She is also the Founder and Executive Director for the non-profit organization, *Voicing Futures*.

# Routledge Research in Arts Education

Books in the series include:

**Making and Relational Creativity**
An Exploration of Relationships that Arise through Creative Practices in Informal Making Spaces
*Lindsey Helen Bennett*

**Engaging Youth in Critical Arts Pedagogies and Creative Research for Social Justice**
Opportunities and Challenges of Arts-based Work and Research with Young People
*Edited by Kristen P. Goessling, Dana E. Wright, Amanda C. Wager and Marit Dewhurst*

**The Value of Drawing Instruction in the Visual Arts and Across Curricula**
Historical and Philosophical Arguments for Drawing in the Digital Age
*Seymour Simmons III*

**Perspectives on Learning Assessment in the Arts in Higher Education**
Supporting Transparent Assessment across Artistic Disciplines
*Edited by Diane Leduc and Sébastien Béland*

**Culturally Sustaining Pedagogies in Music Education**
Expanding Culturally Responsive Teaching to Sustain Diverse Musical Cultures and Identities
*Emily Good-Perkins*

**Addressing Issues of Mental Health in Schools through the Arts**
Teachers and Music Therapists Working Together
*Edited by Jane Tarr and Nick Clough*

# Culturally Sustaining Pedagogies in Music Education

Expanding Culturally Responsive Teaching to Sustain Diverse Musical Cultures and Identities

Emily Good-Perkins

NEW YORK AND LONDON

First published 2022
by Routledge
605 Third Avenue, New York, NY 10158

and by Routledge
2 Park Square, Milton Park, Abingdon, Oxon OX14 4RN

*Routledge is an imprint of the Taylor & Francis Group, an informa business*

© 2022 Emily Good-Perkins

The right of Emily Good-Perkins to be identified as author of this work has been asserted by her in accordance with sections 77 and 78 of the Copyright, Designs and Patents Act 1988.

All rights reserved. No part of this book may be reprinted or reproduced or utilised in any form or by any electronic, mechanical, or other means, now known or hereafter invented, including photocopying and recording, or in any information storage or retrieval system, without permission in writing from the publishers.

*Trademark notice*: Product or corporate names may be trademarks or registered trademarks, and are used only for identification and explanation without intent to infringe.

DOI: 10.4324/9781003099475

*Library of Congress Cataloging-in-Publication Data*
Names: Good-Perkins, Emily, author.
Title: Culturally sustaining pedagogies in music education : expanding culturally responsive teaching to sustain diverse musical cultures and identities / Emily Good-Perkins.
Description: [1.] | New York : Routledge, 2021. |
Series: Routledge research in arts education |
Includes bibliographical references and index.
Identifiers: LCCN 2021018795 | ISBN 9780367568191 (hardback) |
ISBN 9780367568221 (paperback) | ISBN 9781003099475 (ebook)
Subjects: LCSH: Music--Instruction and study. |
Culturally sustaining pedagogy.
Classification: LCC MT1.G615 C85 2021 | DDC 780.71--dc23
LC record available at https://lccn.loc.gov/2021018795

ISBN: 9780367568191 (hbk)
ISBN: 9780367568221 (pbk)
ISBN: 9781003099475 (ebk)

DOI: 10.4324/9781003099475

Typeset in Sabon
by Taylor & Francis Books

This book is dedicated to John, Lili, Noah, Jacob, and Howard and Gloria, without whom this book would have never been possible.

# Contents

| | |
|---|---:|
| *List of Figures* | ix |
| *Acknowledgements* | x |

**PART I**
## Culturally Sustaining Pedagogy       1

| | | |
|---|---|---:|
| 1 | The Importance of Theory | 3 |
| 2 | Why Culturally Sustaining Pedagogy for Music Education? | 10 |

**PART II**
## Historical Overview of Today's Music Classroom       23

| | | |
|---|---|---:|
| 3 | Music and the "Civilizing" Mission | 25 |
| 4 | Music and the "Civilizing" Mission in the United States | 38 |
| 5 | Character Improvement and Music Education in the United States | 53 |
| 6 | Music Education Standardization and Codification | 60 |

**PART III**
## Today's Music Classroom       77

| | | |
|---|---|---:|
| 7 | How Do Our Normalized Practices Impact Children Today? | 79 |
| 8 | Two Music Teaching Approaches | 86 |
| 9 | How Do Students Describe a Meaningful Music Classroom? | 99 |

viii   *Contents*

**PART IV**
**Culturally Sustaining Pedagogy in Music Education**          105

10   Musical Epistemology and Music Education          107


**PART V**
**Moving Forward Towards Culturally Sustaining Music Pedagogy**          125

11   Practical Implications for the Music Classroom          127

12   Towards a Framework for Culturally Sustaining Music
     Pedagogy          140


     *Index*          150

# Figures

4.1 White Buffalo, Cheyenne Nation, 1881 (left); White Buffalo,
    1882 (right)    40
4.2 Tom Torlino, Navajo Nation, 1882 (left); Tom Torlino, 1885
    (right)    41
4.3 Carlisle Indian School Band and Choir    42

# Acknowledgements

An earlier version of Part IV, Chapter 10 appeared in: Good-Perkins, E. (2021). Culturally sustaining music education and epistemic travel. *Philosophy of Music Education Review*, 29(1), 47–66. https://doi.org/10.2979/philmusiedu crevi.29.1.04

Reprinted by permission of the Publisher. From Django Paris and H. Samy Alim, Eds., *Culturally Sustaining Pedagogies: Teaching and Learning for Justice in a Changing World*, New York: Teachers College Press. Copyright © 2017 by Teachers College, Columbia University. All rights reserved.

Carlisle Indian School photographs published courtesy of Carlisle Indian School Digital Resource Center.

Part I

# Culturally Sustaining Pedagogy

# 1 The Importance of Theory

The age-old debate about whether theory is important for practice is one in which immediate teaching needs are weighed against lofty theoretical concepts that may seem to be divorced from reality. The ways in which theory is connected to practice oftentimes seem elusive and impractical. Why should teachers take the time to theorize when the immediate and practical demands of teaching seem to be more pressing? Isn't theory just a distraction from the real work of teaching? What is theory?

In their guide to social justice education entitled *Is Everyone Really Equal*, Sensoy and DiAngelo (2017) argue that theory is always present and cannot be separated from teaching. They describe theory as a person's worldview, which might be "conceptualized as the learned cultural maps we follow to navigate and make sense of our lives and new things we encounter" (p. 28). With every decision they make, teachers subconsciously employ their own theoretical perspectives. Their worldview informs each interaction with their students as well as the ways in which they deliver a pedagogical concept. Teachers' worldviews, whether they are aware of it or not, profoundly impact their students. The study of theory, therefore, allows teachers to become critically conscious of their own theoretical perspectives while deepening their understanding of the ways in which theory can inform their practice. It is the mistaken assumption that theory can be divorced from teaching and the invisibility of our theoretical worldviews that make the study of theory an essential component of music teaching.

In addition to being a means by which to uncover the ideological underpinnings of one's assumptions and actions, theory helps us understand the complex and hegemonic inequality perpetuated in education. In her discussion about abolitionist teaching as a means by which to pursue educational freedom, Love (2019) describes the ways in which theories "work to explain to us how the world works, who the world denies, and how structures uphold oppression" (p. 146). Educators who deny the importance of theory, therefore, might be equated to politicians bemoaning politically correct language or White people claiming to be colorblind. All of these assertions privilege the status quo and those who benefit from mainstream ideology at the expense of the many who are marginalized by it. Theory, therefore,

DOI: 10.4324/9781003099475-2

4 *Culturally Sustaining Pedagogy*

provides a means by which to uncover the ways in which individual and systemic ideology contribute to oppression within education.

Why, then, should teachers investigate their own worldviews and the ways in which theory might inform their teaching? Leonardo and Grubb (2019) argue that racial inequality in American schools is perpetuated because minoritized students' worldviews are not recognized in the classroom. For minoritized students, "schooling has become largely irrelevant to their culture, understanding, and belief systems," and they "experience schooling as largely foreign to their self-concept, a process that neither affirms nor is ultimately useful for them" (p. xiii). For educators to be able to attend to the needs of their students, they must understand the ways in which their theoretical worldview informs their teaching. This is particularly important as the world becomes more interconnected than ever before.

Globalization, mass migration, technology, a global pandemic, and the growing divide between the wealthy and the poor make the need for worldviews in education ever more pressing. In the United States, the percentage of children who are White is less than one half of American children (Vespa et al., 2018, p. 8). This percentage will continue to decline, and by 2060, only one third of American children will be White (p. 4). Similarly, in Canada, as the immigrant population continues to increase, it is projected that by 2036, "between 44.2% and 49.7%" of the population will be composed of "immigrants and second-generation individuals" (Morency et al., 2017, p. 6). In the UK, 73 percent of the population growth between 2018 and 2028 will be attributed to the growing immigrant population (Nash, 2019, p. 2).

The growing diversity is perhaps most visible in school classrooms where the rich cultural, musical, and linguistic diversity of these changing populations is present and vibrant. Diverse student populations require that educators approach their teaching in ways that affirm all students. Theoretical perspectives or worldviews allow teachers to approach their teaching equitably and in ways that are relevant for their students. This is particularly important for music educators, as music and culture are so intimately intertwined and, for many students, constitute an important part of their identities (Good-Perkins, 2020).

## Culturally Relevant and Responsive Pedagogies

Within the United States, educational theories and the belief systems in which they are entangled have informed the ways in which children of color are approached and taught in the classroom. Prior to the 1970s, deficit educational models deemed cultures outside of White mainstream society a detriment to education. Children of color with rich cultural lives and vibrant communities were forced to ignore their cultural ways of being and knowing in the classroom. The underpinning motive of this educational model was for children to abandon their cultures as a means to succeed in mainstream American society. The aim of deficit approaches, according to Paris (2012), was to replace "the linguistic, literate, and cultural practices many students of color brought from their homes and communities ... with what were viewed as superior practices" (p. 93).

In the 1970s and 1980s, deficit educational models gave way to *difference approaches* (Paris, 2012, p. 94) where children of color's cultures were recognized but remained inappropriate for educational settings. Both deficit and difference educational models positioned students' cultural competencies outside the realm of academic success. During this time, the devaluation of children's cultural identities within educational settings galvanized new educational scholarship on culture and learning and the ways in which children's cultural identities could be valued and used in the classroom. These approaches, described as *resource pedagogies* (p. 94), honored children's cultural backgrounds as a means by which to access dominant, mainstream knowledge.

It was within this educational climate and as a criticism of educational research, at the time, that "fail[ed] to make explicit its theoretical underpinnings" (Ladson-Billings, 1995, p. 469) that Ladson-Billings first proposed her theory of *culturally relevant pedagogy*. She argued that the absence of theoretical clarity did not result in an absence of theory but rather allowed for a *default theory* assumed to be objective and therefore unquestioned. Ladson-Billings emphasized the ways in which a new theoretical paradigm provides a lens, or worldview, through which to view educational research and practice. It was in defiance of the deficit worldview and approach to teaching African American children that Ladson-Billings (1995) introduced her theory of culturally relevant pedagogy, which she defined as a "theoretical model that not only addresses student achievement but also helps students to accept and affirm their cultural identity while developing critical perspectives that challenge inequities that schools (and other institutions) perpetuate" (p. 469).

Ladson-Billings (1995) recognized the need for reforms within teacher education so as to better prepare teachers for socially just and equitable teaching. Her study of successful teachers of African American students provided a foundation for her theory. She observed that these teachers used different strategies to achieve success. By deducing commonalities amongst these teachers, she formed the theoretical underpinnings for culturally relevant pedagogy. The successful teachers helped their students become "academically successful, culturally competent, and socio-politically critical" (p. 477). *Academic success* refers to the student's intellectual growth in response to the teacher's instruction and approach (Ladson-Billings, 2014). *Cultural competence* describes the student's awareness and appreciation of her culture of origin while simultaneously learning about other cultures. *Socio-political consciousness* refers to the student's ability to critically analyze social and political systems and policies. Ladson-Billings' three tenets of culturally relevant pedagogy provided a theoretical foundation for researchers in educational justice.

## 6 *Culturally Sustaining Pedagogy*

Influenced by Ladson-Billings' theory, Gay (2000) proposed five elements of *culturally responsive teaching* as a pedagogy for pre-service education programs. She recognized that teacher education programs were advocating for multicultural education but failing to provide their students with the necessary skills to succeed. Much like Ladson-Billings, Gay used the experiences and stories of teachers working with African American, Latinx, Asian American, and Native American students as data (Gay, 2002). In addition, her other data sources consisted of research and theory pertaining to multicultural education from multiple disciplines including: K-12 teachers, university professors, sociologists, anthropologists, and psychologists to inform her research on culturally responsive pedagogy. She defined culturally responsive teaching as,

> using the cultural characteristics, experiences, and perspectives of ethnically diverse students as conduits for teaching them more effectively …. As a result, the academic achievement of ethnically diverse students will improve when they are taught through their own cultural and experiential filters.
>
> (Gay, 2002, p. 106)

Gay, among others, developed and furthered Ladson-Billings' theory so that it evolved into new forms and interpretations. In 2014, Ladson-Billings stated: "my work on culturally relevant pedagogy has taken on a life of its own, and what I see in the literature and sometimes in practice is totally unrecognizable to me" (p. 82). Due to the liberty with which Ladson-Billings' initial ideas were applied, 20 years after the development of her theory, *culturally relevant pedagogy*, Ladson-Billings (2014) called for a "remix" (p. 76). She recognized the important influence her 1995 theory had on research pertaining to culturally relevant and responsive pedagogies and the many paths which diverged from her initial three tenets. However, because of the fluidity of scholarship and the dynamic nature of culture, Ladson-Billings believed a remix was necessary.

The approach for which Ladson-Billings advocated was developed by Paris (2012) in response to a changing society. Paris argued that the terms *relevant* and *responsive* do not adequately address the needs of a pluralistic society. These terms refer to the way in which a student's culture is used to teach him the dominant culture. Paris proposed *culturally sustaining pedagogy* (CSP) as an alternative. CSP aims to perpetuate and encourage cultural plurality. This pedagogical stance is strongly supportive of students' cultures rather than merely responsive or relevant. CSP seeks to sustain culture both in a traditional and evolving way according to students' lived experiences by "support [ing] young people in sustaining the cultural and linguistic competence of their communities while simultaneously offering access to dominant cultural competence" (Paris, 2012, p. 95). Paris introduced the term *culturally sustaining pedagogy* as both a concept and social commitment, and this led to future research and advocacy in the pursuance of educational justice.

## Culturally Sustaining Pedagogies

Paris and Alim's (2017) compilation of scholarship on culturally sustaining pedagogies expands Paris' (2012) discussion to include a variety of critical viewpoints. In their "loving critique" (Paris & Alim, 2017, p. 4) of asset pedagogies, Paris and Alim call for a radical departure from neo-liberal approaches to educational equity. They emphasize the need for a stance where students' "funds of knowledge" (González et al., 2005) are recognized and valued unto themselves and not merely as a means to teach the dominant epistemology. This conception is in direct opposition to normative educational practices because it requires a heterogenous approach to culture, language, and pedagogy: "By proposing schooling as a site for sustaining the cultural ways of being of communities of color rather than eradicating them, CSP is responding to the many ways that schools continue to function as part of the colonial project" (Paris & Alim, 2017, p. 2).

Similarly, Domínguez (2017), who adds "revitalization" to Paris' conception of cultural sustenance, emphasizes the need for a decolonization of teacher education, where teachers engage in "epistemic travel" (p. 225) as a means of disrupting harmful dominant discourses and closing the "ontological distance" that alienates teachers from students. He states that "colonization as an explicit *de jure* system of political domination has ended, yes. Yet bans on ethnic studies ... and assaults on agency, culture, language, and identity persist. These are the accruing injuries of coloniality" (p. 227). The "assaults on agency, culture, language, and identity" about which Domínguez speaks is further articulated by Bucholtz et al. (2017) in their discussion about language agency. They assert that "one of the most important yet most devalued resources available to youth of color is their language" (p. 44). For Paris and Alim (2017), the recognition of linguistic plurality in educational settings is a crucial component of CSP. Language agency is further examined by Rosa and Flores (2017) from a "critical raciolinguistic perspective" (p. 186). In their discussion about discourses of "appropriateness," they argue for a dismantling of the linguistic hierarchy that continues to marginalize students of color. Educators who enact CSP allow for and value the linguistic practices of their students. They do so by actively working to disrupt "linguistic purity" discourses (p. 185).

The linguistic and cultural heritage of students of color is at the center of CSP. In her discussion about intergenerational cultural practices, Lee (2017) expands the discussion about "emergent" and "heritage" (Domínguez, 2017, p. 233) cultural practices within CSP. One of the tenets of CSP is that culture is fluid and changeable and thus students' cultural practices should not be essentialized. However, within the emergent forms of culture, both Lee and Paris emphasize the importance of recognizing heritage practices. Lee (2017) calls them a "repository of historically intergenerational cultural practices" (p. 266). It is the simultaneous recognition of both heritage and emergent cultural practices in a non-binary and non-essentializing way that

## 8  Culturally Sustaining Pedagogy

allows for students' cultural identities to flourish. This, however, according to Lee, is also the "dilemma" without a "simple resolution" but "is a necessary first step" (p. 268). She states that "as we think about what should be sustained and why, we must realize that there are always competing demands around what is historically transmitted as tradition, and new practices and allegiances that are often hybrid and emergent" (p. 268). Despite the dilemma, the recognition of students' cultures both in traditional and evolving ways is an important step towards culturally sustaining and revitalizing education.

The aspects of CSP on which Paris and Alim (2017) and the contributing scholars focused—cultural plurality, coloniality in education, discourses of "appropriateness," linguistic and cultural competence, and emergent and historical practices—are all applicable to music education and will be further explored throughout this book.

## References

Bucholtz, M., Casillas, D. I., & Lee, J. S. (2017). Language and culture as sustenance. In D. Paris & H.S. Alim (Eds.), *Culturally sustaining pedagogies: Teaching and learning for justice in a changing world* (pp. 43–59). Teachers College Press.

Domínguez, M. (2017). "Se hace puentes al andar:" Decolonial teacher education as a needed bridge to culturally sustaining and revitalizing pedagogies. In D. Paris & H. S. Alim (Eds.), *Culturally sustaining pedagogies: Teaching and learning for justice in a changing world* (pp. 225–245). Teachers College Press.

Gay, G. (2000). *Culturally responsive teaching: Theory, research, and practice.* Teachers College Press.

Gay, G. (2002). Preparing for culturally responsive teaching. *Journal of Teacher Education, 53*(2), 106–116. doi:10.1177/0022487102053002003.

González, N., Moll, L. C., & Amanti, C. (Eds.). (2005). *Funds of knowledge: Theorizing practices in households, communities, and classrooms.* Routledge. doi:10.4324/9781410613462.

Good-Perkins, E. (2020). Rethinking vocal education as a means to encourage positive identity development in adolescents. In I. M. Yob & E. R. Jorgensen (Eds.), *Humane music education for the common good* (pp. 158–171). Indiana University Press. doi:10.2307/j.ctvxcrxmm.

Ladson-Billings, G. (1995). Toward a theory of culturally relevant pedagogy. *American Educational Research Journal, 32*(3), 465–491. doi:10.3102/00028312032003465.

Ladson-Billings, G. (2014). Culturally relevant pedagogy 2.0: A.k.a. the remix. *Harvard Educational Review, 84*(1), 74–84. doi:10.17763/haer.84.1.p2rj131485484751.

Lee, C. D. (2017). An ecological framework for enacting culturally sustaining pedagogy. In D. Paris & H. S. Alim (Eds.), *Culturally sustaining pedagogies: Teaching and learning for justice in a changing world* (pp. 261–273). Teachers College Press.

Leonardo, Z., & Grubb, W. N. (2019). *Education and racism: A primer on issues and dilemmas.* (2nd ed.). Routledge. doi:10.4324/9781315101200.

Love, B. L. (2019). *We want to do more than survive: Abolitionist teaching and the pursuit of educational freedom.* Beacon Press.

Morency, J. D., Caron-Malenfant, É., & MacIsaac, S. (2017). Immigration and diversity: Population projections for Canada and its Regions, 2011 to 2036. Statistics Canada= Statistique Canada. Retrieved from https://www150.statcan.gc.ca/n1/pub/91-551-x/91-551-x2017001-eng.htm.

Nash, A. (2019). National population projections: 2018-based. Office for National Statistics, United Kingdom. Retrieved from https://www.ons.gov.uk/peoplepopulationandcommunity/populationandmigration/populationprojections/bulletins/nationalpopulationprojections/2018based.

Paris, D. (2012). Culturally sustaining pedagogy: A needed change in stance, terminology, and practice. *Educational Researcher*, 41(3), 93–97. doi:10.3102/0013189x12441244.

Paris, D., & Alim, H. S. (Eds.). (2017). *Culturally sustaining pedagogies: Teaching and learning for justice in a changing world*. Teachers College Press.

Rosa, J., & Flores, N. (2017). Do you hear what I hear? Raciolinguistic ideologies and culturally sustaining pedagogies. In D. Paris & H. S. Alim (Eds.), *Culturally sustaining pedagogies: Teaching and learning for justice in a changing world* (pp. 175–190). Teachers College Press.

Sensoy, O., & DiAngelo, R. (2017). *Is everyone really equal?: An introduction to key concepts in social justice education*. Teachers College Press.

Vespa, J., Medina, L., & Armstrong, D. M. (2018). *Demographic turning points for the United States: Population projections for 2020 to 2060*. Washington, DC: US Department of Commerce, Economics and Statistics Administration, US Census Bureau.

# 2 Why Culturally Sustaining Pedagogy for Music Education?

Many of the normalized values and assumptions found in Western classical music education, which permeates both Western and non-Western music classrooms, are tied to racist and colonial histories. These assumptions are perpetuated because of *colonial-blind, color-blind*, and *universalist* beliefs that Western classical music and the performance practices, aesthetics, and values with which it is associated can transcend differences of race, culture, and worldview (Benedict, 2009; Bradley, 2015; Calderon, 2011; Gould, 2012; Gustafson, 2009). Students for whom a Eurocentric musical epistemology is not relevant receive and internalize an implicit message based upon the absence of their own musical epistemologies in the music classroom, that their musical worldviews are inappropriate for this particular music setting. This silencing is visceral and a violent rejection of students' musical-cultural identities.

## Culturally Responsive Music Education

Within the field of music education, scholars have addressed culture in the music classroom. Gay's conception of culturally responsive pedagogy, defined "as using the cultural characteristics, experiences, and perspectives of ethnically diverse students as conduits for teaching them more effectively" (Gay, 2002, p. 106) has provided inspiration for scholarship on culturally responsive music education.

Using a multiple embedded case study design, Shaw (2014) studied the application of culturally responsive pedagogy with three choirs from an urban children's choir organization. She was particularly interested in the students' perceptions of culturally responsive pedagogy. In addition, she explored the relationship between the students' cultural and musical identities and the ways in which culturally responsive pedagogy bridges gaps between home and school cultures. Shaw discovered that the culturally responsive instruction fostered, what Gay (2002) has called "pedagogical bridges" (p. 113) between the students' school life and family life. This in turn helped to strengthen the students' cultural identities and encourage familial involvement (Shaw, 2019, p. 81).

DOI: 10.4324/9781003099475-3

Similarly, Abril (2013), in his discussion about a culturally responsive general music classroom, suggested ways in which teachers might connect musical elements and classroom knowledge with music that is experienced outside of the classroom by "help[ing] students make connections between the music being studied or performed in the classroom and the musical world beyond the classroom" (p. 9). Abril suggests that teachers draw "explicit connection[s] between the use of a given musical element (e.g., gradual crescendo) and the emotion that its use in a composition might evoke" (p. 9).

Lind and McKoy (2016) discuss the ways in which culturally responsive pedagogy, in theory and practice, can be applied to music teaching and learning. Drawing from Gay's (2010) theoretical framework, they assert that "culturally responsive teaching implies the ability to affirm diverse cultural characteristics, perspectives, and experiences and to use these multiple perceptions of reality and ways of knowing to form bridges to new learning and ideas" (Lind & McKoy, 2016, p. 17). In line with Gay's conception of culturally responsive pedagogy, Lind and McKoy emphasize the ways in which culturally responsive music teaching recognizes students' cultural identities and bridges home and school cultures. In doing so, music educators can more effectively teach their musical curriculum.

The vignettes in Lind and McKoy's (2016) book provide a glimpse into the lives of music teachers who are carefully considering and discerning the ways in which they can be more culturally responsive in their teaching. Creatively, they are re-thinking their curricular, pedagogical, and musical ways of being in the classroom in response to their students. As music teachers, their teacher education emphasized musical norms, many of which they were now reconsidering.

> There is a self-perpetuating model of music education that maintains a traditional approach ... method books that are commonly available often connect directly to traditional Western instruments and are based on symphonic band, concert choir, and string orchestra models of instruction. Michael recognized this and described how, as a culturally responsive teacher, he had to challenge the traditional perceptions promoted in commercially advertised instructional materials.
>
> (Lind & McKoy, 2016, p. 95)

In their synthesis of the teachers' accounts, Lind and McKoy (2016) recognized that teachers who wanted to enact culturally responsive music teaching had to create new curriculum and strategies and were consistently challenging the normalized music teacher education paradigm. Similarly, Abril, in his (2009) discussion about what it means to be culturally responsive in an instrumental music program, also concluded that the dominant music education paradigm found in music teacher education programs and enacted by teachers in K-12 classrooms limited culturally responsive music education and created a "disconnect" (p. 79) between students and teachers.

## 12  *Culturally Sustaining Pedagogy*

### Refusing the "White Gaze"

This re-thinking of pedagogy, curriculum, repertoire, ensemble structures, and expectations begs the question, whom does music teacher education serve? White teachers in White schools? In our discussions about cultural relevance and responsiveness, we will continue to perpetuate the same systems of exclusion if we do not center these discussions on the implicit and explicit racism inherent in the curriculum and belief systems of music education.

Using Morrison's (1998) conception of the "White gaze," Paris and Alim (2017) shed light on the ways in which whiteness permeates educational research and practice, and the ways in which educational success is defined as "a unidirectional assimilation into whiteness" (p. 3). Drawing from Morrison's refusal of the White gaze in her writing, they ask:

> What can educators of color and other educators in solidarity with us learn from Morrison's courage and conviction to de-center whiteness, to envision a world where we owed no explanations to White people about the value of our children's culture, language and learning potential?
>
> (Paris & Alim, 2017, p. 3)

By refusing the White gaze in music education, we commit to knowing, loving, and empowering children of color within all aspects of music teaching and learning, beginning with teacher education. What would music teacher education look like if the default student for whom the curriculum and teaching were geared was Black or Brown rather than just White? How can we change the narrative from musical saviorism in which we use children's cultures as a bridge to the dominant musical curriculum to musical sustenance in which children's musical cultures *are* the curriculum? Music teaching and curriculum that refuse the White gaze are rooted in children's musical cultures. This type of teaching does not require a bridge because it allows children of color's musical competence to *be* the curriculum. Paris and Alim (2017) argue that:

> For too long, scholarship on "access" and "equity" has centered implicitly or explicitly around the White-gaze-centered question: How can "we" get "these" working-class kids of color to speak/write/be more like middle-class White ones (rather than critiquing the White gaze itself that sees, hears, and frames students of color in everywhichway as marginal and deficient)?
>
> (Paris & Alim, 2017, p. 3)

What are the "White-gaze-centered" questions within the field of music education that are posited as justice-seeking but in fact reinstate dominant hierarchies of power and knowledge? Rather than merely responding to children's musical ways of knowing, culturally sustaining music pedagogy *is* children's musical way of knowing. Culturally sustaining pedagogy recognizes students' musical cultures as entities unto themselves which should be celebrated, sustained, resurrected, and revitalized in the music classroom.

In his discussion about cultural responsiveness in an instrumental music program, Abril (2009) illuminates the ways in which a Mariachi ensemble is important for some Chicanx communities as a symbol of Mexican heritage and nationalism as well as "vocational training" (p. 80). Thus, school musical opportunities that build students' cultural competence allow students to actively contribute to and sustain the musical cultures of their community. In Sleeter's (2018) discussion about the future of multicultural education, she emphasizes that "many minoritized communities want their youth to become not only proud of their cultural and language background, but also able to function well within their cultural communities" (p. 16).

Culturally sustaining pedagogy requires that educators challenge the White gaze in teaching and research. By doing so, racist structures and practices can be revealed and dismantled. Within the field of music education, the seemingly innocent emphasis on standards, musical literacy, and the elements of music, among other things, have provided a neo-liberal glossing over of the ways in which these goals and their Eurocentric origins allow for perpetuated racism. Of course, musical standards are good. Why would a teacher or music teacher education program say otherwise? Why shouldn't we emphasize the elements of music and musical literacy? The inherent problem with this discourse is that it implicitly privileges the Western classical music knowledge system thereby deeming "bridges" necessary. Children, whose musical cultures fall outside of the Western classical epistemology, come to believe that their musical cultures are only important enough as a bridge to more appropriate school knowledge. In this form, culturally responsive music teaching, therefore, allows for the reproduction of hierarchical relationships between dominant knowledge systems—reinforced in school settings—and the knowledge systems of students' cultural and familial backgrounds.

## The "New Mainstream"

In addition to the specific content emphasized within a Western classical paradigm, the ways of thinking within this paradigm themselves hinder authentic and equitable music teaching. Fixed notions of musical culture, whether they be musical scores, music theory, or music history, have and continue to provide the foundation for most music teaching and learning in the United States and beyond. Typically, framed within the Western classical paradigm, a canon provides a foundation for teacher education, confidence for pre-service teachers, and predictability across the field of teaching and learning music. Therefore, it is difficult for a field whose identity is based on fixed notions of culture to envision teaching music in any other way.

## 14 *Culturally Sustaining Pedagogy*

It is because of this pedagogical epistemology—we teach from fixed scores, like Schubert's "Die Forelle"; established methods, like Orff and Kodály; fixed theoretical concepts, like Schenkerian analysis—on which music education is grounded that the adoption of music equity within the music classroom has fallen short. Certainly, music educators at all levels have aspired to incorporate Arabic folk song, African drumming, body percussion, and hip hop. Oftentimes, unfortunately, what is implemented in the music classroom is in fact a fixed notion of culture, sometimes unrecognizable to students for whom the culture is in fact relevant. The problem, therefore, is not that teachers do not have access to relevant resources or that teachers are not creative enough to discover more relevant musical options. The problem, rather, is that the field is defined by and continues to perpetuate the assumption that musical culture can be fixed, preserved, and taught in the music classroom much like a Brahms symphony or a Beethoven sonata.

Using culturally sustaining pedagogy as a framework, Paris (2012) implores educators to interrogate fixed and essentialized notions of culture and actively work to incorporate and recognize the ways in which culture is fluid, ever changing, and evident in hybrid forms in the classroom and in our students' lives. Culturally sustaining pedagogy requires that we deepen our analysis of that which has come before to better expand and respond to the students of today and tomorrow. Therefore, as we move forward as a field to better serve the needs of our students, not only must we dismantle the Western classical hierarchy in order to allow for diverse musical epistemologies, we must find ways to change the mindset that provides the foundation for all musical teaching and learning. How might we move from a fixed notion of culture to one that is fluid, adaptable, ever-changing; one that values the person, the student, the teacher over the score and the method? Might we allow a Mozart score to be changed? Might we allow our methods to be combined, mashed up, and regurgitated into new and hybrid forms? Shouldn't hybridity, fluidity, and creativity be the first notions that come to mind when discussing music education? Shouldn't we strive for creative liberation, self-expression, and imagination rather than standards, methods, and the worship of scores?

After all, as Paris (2015) assures us, this is not only equitable, but the way of the future. The "new mainstream" (p. 222) is not monocultural, mono-lingual, or mono-musical but rather a culturally rich depiction of the world at large. All students will be better equipped to navigate the rapidly diversifying, globalized world, if their education embraces pluralistic and hybrid outcomes. Paris and Alim remind us that:

> We can no longer assume that the White, middle-class linguistic, literate, and cultural skills and ways of being that were considered the sole gatekeepers ... will remain so as our society changes. CSP, then, is increasingly needed not only to promote equality ... but also to ensure access and opportunity.
>
> (Paris & Alim, 2014, p. 89)

Culturally sustaining pedagogy (CSP), therefore, is centered on cultural plurality in the classroom where all students' "funds of knowledge" (González et al., 2005) are taught. How can music education actively resist a mono-musical educational paradigm? By actively working to teach culturally plural music epistemologies in the classroom, we are attending to what Paris calls "the project of social and cultural justice" (Paris, 2012, p. 96), or what we might call "musical justice."

## "Epistemologies of Ignorance"

A music teaching epistemology that is centered on cultural, social, and musical justice is one that is rooted in the musical lives of our students, which, as Paris (2012) contends, are fluid, hybrid, flexible yet connected to heritage musical practices. The type of musical epistemology that would allow for such complexity, diversity, and fluidity in the music classroom is one that is not devoted to a canon but rather—as described by McLaren in his preface to Malewski and Jaramillo's (2011) discussion about "epistemologies of ignorance"—"an epistemology of decolonialism that is not monological, monotopic, or imperial and that does not dilute the particular into the same .... We need, rather, a diversality, a pluriversal universal" (p. xiv). The epistemic expansion necessary for culturally sustaining pedagogy requires that we address the ways in which our "ignorance" or "unknowing" of diverse musical epistemologies is in fact an active erasure and silencing of those epistemologies.

Malewski and Jaramillo (2011) reveal how "ignorance, as the active production of 'unknowing' ... keep[s] in motion 'the way things are' instead of thinking about 'the ways things could be'" (p. 2). Similarly, Paris (2019) considers the ways in which this active "unknowing" has prevented educational reform movements from making lasting change. Although couched in social justice, these reforms have ignored the salience of race and racism and continued to name children of color deficiently, albeit with different names. Paris describes the naming of students of color with terms like "'urban,' 'diverse,' 'minority,' 'underserved,' 'at-risk' and so many terms" as an "avoidance of the prominence of race, racialization, and racism"—an "erasure" that allows for the perpetuation of "beliefs in the superiority of White, middle-class, monolingual, cis-hetero-patriarchal-ableist ways of being at the expense of all others" (Paris, 2019, p. 218).

For many educational initiatives that focus on equity and diversity, the rationale for doing so is to address the "achievement gap." This goal, however, perpetuates discourses of deficiency, oftentimes along lines of ethnicity and socioeconomics. Rather than interrogate the ways in which education continues to expect Black and Brown children to adopt White, normalized "standards" of language and culture (music included) at the expense of their own, discussions about closing the achievement gap deem Black and Brown children's cultures inadequate for educational settings and outcomes. CSP

16   *Culturally Sustaining Pedagogy*

calls for a shift in focus, a change in vantage point. What if the achievement gap were in fact the gaps and epistemologies of ignorance perpetuated by our educational systems? Perhaps the gaps lie in our teaching methods, curriculum, repertoire, and pedagogy rather than in students' achievement.

Paris and Alim (2017) and other scholars who advocate for CSP (Domínguez, 2017; Lee, 2017; Rosa & Flores, 2017) assert that terms like "bridge," "achievement gap," inclusive, diverse, urban, amongst others, are coded terms used to marginalize and pathologize children of color. Rather than attend to inequity, this language perpetuates the hierarchy of knowledge systems and continues to blame children for whom those dominant knowledge systems— Dominant American English (Paris & Alim, 2017, p. 6) and Western classical music standards—are unfamiliar. This language perpetuates White superiority, is rooted in colonialist history, and reifies musical and educational saviorism. In other words, because the accepted curriculum, musical ways of being, and language in educational institutions remain unquestioned, the position will continue to be one of assimilationism—the marginalized conforming to that which is deemed educationally "appropriate." Discourses of appropriateness in language study, much like music, allow certain knowledge systems to be privileged and implicitly considered more "pure" than others.

> Linguistic purity—like racial purity—is a powerful ideological construct. We should seek to understand the perspectives from which such forms of purity and impurity are constructed and perceived rather than focusing on the forms themselves.
>
> (Paris & Alim, 2017, p. 185)

Culturally sustaining pedagogy calls for educators to incorporate children's cultural knowledge systems in all aspects of the curriculum. This requires a dismantling of that which we consider appropriate or inappropriate for the classroom and a recognition of children's musical cultures as ends unto themselves. From this vantage point, all knowledge systems and cultural ways of being are appropriate for school settings. For example, Rosa and Flores (2017) suggest:

> What if culturally specific Spanish language use in everyday Latinx communities were incorporated into all aspects of the curriculum? These shifts would allow us to reimagine the Spanish language skills Estela learned at home and in the community as central to her educational success rather than as starting points from which to learn "legitimate" Spanish.
>
> (pp. 185–186)

## Listening and Whiteness

By attending to the epistemic "gaps" in our curriculum and pedagogy, we can centralize children's musical cultures within all aspects of our music classrooms. This, however, is merely the first step in advocating for educational justice in our schools. Rosa and Flores (2017) extend their discussion about raciolinguistic ideologies further and argue that a true reckoning with racio-linguistic ideologies—what we might extend to raciomusical ideologies—requires a radical shift in perspective. Much like the earlier discussion about the White gaze, Rosa and Flores argue that the White ear determines whether Black and Brown bodies' linguistic competence is deemed appropriate irre-spective of the sound they produce. Therefore, language, even if it is considered to be perfectly spoken Dominant American English, is racialized and judged based upon the body or mouth from which it was spoken.

> We are not suggesting that people from racialized or language-minor-itized communities should not seek to engage in linguistic practices deemed appropriate by mainstream society. However, we contend that the question of whether members of racialized communities are accep-ted as appropriately engaging in these linguistic practices continues to be determined by the White listening subject, not by the speakers' actual practices.
>
> (Paris & Alim, 2017, p. 186)

White listening, therefore, is entangled with the White gaze and in more covert ways allows for the racialization and marginalization of children of color. Within the field of music education, how does White listening impact children of color in the music classroom? Are Black and Brown children, even if they perform perfectly the musical exercise or song, considered less talented than their White classmates? If such racialized listening does take place in the music classroom, are we even aware of it? Are we aware of our own biased listening? This is particularly salient as White teachers are the overwhelming majority even as K-12 student demographics become increas-ingly diverse.

Along the same lines as Rosa and Flores' (2017) discussion of culturally sustaining pedagogy as a means to dismantle raciolingustic ideologies, Stoever (2016) and Eidsheim (2019) examine the ways in which listening and sound are entangled with whiteness and racism. Both Stoever and Eidsheim contend, much like the scholars advocating for CSP, that it is impossible to reveal the pervasiveness of whiteness in musical listening if done so within the same musical framework. Put another way, they were only able to uncover the ways in which listening—the appraisal of sound—contributes to racism because their inquiries were multi-epistemic and multi-disciplinarian. Stoever describes this methodology as "a strategy of critical sonar to navigate the epistemological terrain that 'music'— as a culturally specific, politically charged, and 'entrenched' category of value—can obscure" (Stoever, 2016, p. 18). Stoever goes on to say "the history of the sonic color line and the listening ear should compel scholars to ques-tion music's cultural and institutional privilege" (p. 18).

## 18 *Culturally Sustaining Pedagogy*

Similarly, Eidsheim (2019), who sought to expose the ways in which classical voice teachers, among others, perpetuate the myth that a person's ethnicity can be heard in her vocal timbre, sheds light on the ways scholarship about the voice is segmented amongst different disciplines: "such as (to mention a few) musicology, ethnomusicology, anthropology, film, gender, and sound studies on the one hand; linguistics, biology and evolutionary studies, acoustics, mechanical engineering, and head and neck surgery on the other" (p. 15). The segmentation of voice research amongst multiple disciplines allows each to be epistemologically ignorant of the other and creates what Eidsheim describes as a "roadblock" (p. 14). "As a result of their assumed ontologies, epistemologies, and research methodologies, each of these positions yields distinct, often non-overlapping, voice objects" (pp. 15–16).

Therefore, Eidsheim (2019) and Stoever (2016) call for an epistemic expansion and cross-disciplinary approach to reveal the ways in which our paradigm limits our understanding and allows our "unknowing." This epistemic expansion requires a refocusing, a cross examination of the listening subject, the listening ear, and the ways in which the listening subject perpetuates colonial unknowing in our practices and pedagogies.

> Examining one's listening practices and challenging their predisposed affects, reactions, and interpretations are fundamental for the development of new ways of being in the world and for forging crossracial solidarities capable of dismantling the sonic color line and the racialized listening practices enabling and enabled by it …. Decolonizing begins at colonization, and listening, in particular, is an important method to access freedom, agency, power, and selfhood.
>
> (Stoever, 2016, p. 20)

Eidsheim's (2019) discussion focuses on the racialization of the voice and the role the listening subject plays in perpetuating essentialized notions about the voice. For Eidsheim, all listening is based upon context and culture, and should be approached from a socio-cultural perspective with which power dynamics are also entangled.

> Listening is never neutral, but rather always actively produces meaning, it is a political act. Through listening, we name and define. We get to say, "This is the voice of a black man." We get to say, "That singer doesn't sound sincere." And we get to say, "This singer doesn't sound like herself" … through listening we enact and activate.
>
> (Eidsheim, 2019, p. 24)

The appraisal of sound is an enactment of power—the listener's power to impose upon the sound producer pre-conceived assumptions about sound and who is entitled to produce particular sounds—whether the sound producer is a singer, violinist, drummer, or hip hop artist. This power inevitably

## Why CSP for Music Education? 19

manifests in racialized listening and racialized conceptions of what sound is "appropriate" and "inappropriate" from particular bodies. Within a Western classical paradigm, listening to and appraising the sound we hear are essential components of music teaching. Within this paradigm, listening is considered mostly objective. Did I hear the correct pitch and vowel? Did they play the right notes and dynamics? Drawing from Eidsheim's (2019) and Stoever's (2016) analyses, however, how might our beliefs about objective listening be hindered by the confines of our culturally specific epistemology? How do our beliefs about appropriate and inappropriate sound hinder our ability to hear our students? Singing and the voice are integral components of music education. Is our narrowly focused discernment of the voice preventing students from being fully heard and valued? As a field, does our Eurocentric classical voice pedagogy perpetuate our ignorance of the ways in which we allow for and even disseminate the racist thinking that voices are racialized—that a person's ethnicity determines his or her voice timbre? What other racialized beliefs about music do we unknowingly perpetuate? Do we believe that certain ethnicities are better equipped for particular band or orchestra instruments? Do we try to convince our Black and Brown students to choose particular instruments based on their black and brown bodies?

CSP calls us to question the White gaze and the White listening ear, which invisibly define the ways in which we view and appraise our students. In what ways are our beliefs about our students based on racist and colonial histories? How do those beliefs manifest in the music classroom? Do we recognize our students' musical competence as essential knowledge in our music classrooms, or do we perpetuate discourses of musical superiority and musical hierarchy? How might we shift our focus on deficiencies from students to the deficiencies and achievement gaps in our music teaching and curriculum? Because our musical practices and pedagogies are, for the most part, based solely on one specific paradigm, how do we even begin to reconceptualize our teaching?

### Closing the Ontological Distance and Embracing a New Paradigm

For Domínguez (2017), culturally sustaining pedagogy requires that teachers eradicate coloniality in their practices and beliefs and rethink their teaching from the vantage point of their students rather than their own.

> Ultimately, we need a decolonizing teacher education pedagogy, one that centers itself—intentionally and intensely—on the humanity and possibility of students of color, and on dismantling the accepted logics and prevailing discourses of coloniality that only highlight their "otherness".
> (Domínguez, 2017, p. 232)

This pedagogical stance disrupts coloniality by "closing the ontological distance" between teachers and students requiring that teachers humanize,

## 20 *Culturally Sustaining Pedagogy*

care for, and know their students. A decolonial, culturally sustaining pedagogy requires that teachers be epistemically adventuresome, creative, and courageous. This pedagogical stance requires a new vantage point, a broader epistemic understanding, and cannot take place within the same epistemic paradigm.

Culturally sustaining music pedagogy, therefore, if enacted within a Western classical framework, will continue to perpetuate coloniality. Instead, CSP in music education requires humility and a willingness to concede expertise and the traditional master apprentice model. As we strive to disrupt discourses of appropriateness, linguistic and musical hierarchies, deficit language like "urban" and "achievement gap," and racist ideologies in our curriculum and practice, we must center the cultural knowledge and values of our students while reconciling the ways in which the White gaze and the White listening ear have allowed for the racialization of children of color in the music classroom.

The prioritization of a Eurocentric musical epistemology within the field of music education excludes and silences students for whom this epistemology is not relevant. Despite scholarship on culturally responsive music education (Fitzpatrick, 2012; Lind & McKoy, 2016; Shaw, 2014), in the United States music education is largely the same as it was 50 years ago when the Tanglewood Symposium (Choate et al., 1967) addressed diversity. Within the broader field of education, Paris (2012) conceived of *culturally sustaining pedagogy* in response to a similar conundrum—the neo-liberalization of equity and social justice practices in education. He argued that, rather than radically change the educational climate for marginalized students, discourses about culture and relevance had reinstated the dominant hierarchy. Therefore, Paris and Alim (2017) and others (Bucholtz et al., 2017; Domínguez, 2017; Ladson-Billings, 2014; Lee, 2017) proposed a decolonial, radical pedagogy that recognizes students' cultures as life-giving entities unto themselves and not merely a bridge for teaching dominant culture. In addition, they emphasized both the changing or "emergent" (Domínguez, 2017, p. 233) nature of culture as well as the historical "heritage" (p. 233) and "intergenerational cultural practices" (Lee, 2017, p. 266).

Although music has played an important role in many historical and emergent intergenerational cultural practices for minoritized communities, the musical practices that have sustained and continue to sustain those communities are not often recognized within school music classrooms. Instead, the practices that *are* emphasized, shaped by the Western classical canon, stem from the notion that music epistemology is universal. This framework excludes non-Eurocentric conceptions of musical embodiment, expression, and vocality allowing for the silencing and racializing of student bodies in the classroom. Therefore, to address the exclusion that continues to take place in music classrooms, this book offers a new theoretical and pedagogical framework of *culturally sustaining music pedagogy* based upon Paris' (2012) theoretical framework of *culturally sustaining pedagogy*.

## References

Abril, C. (2009). Responding to culture in the instrumental music programme: A teacher's journey. *Music Education Research*, 11(1), 77–91. doi:10.1080/14613800802699176.

Abril, C. (2013). Toward a more culturally responsive general music classroom. *General Music Today*, 27(1), 6–11. doi:10.1177/1048371313478946.

Benedict, C. (2009). Processes of alienation: Marx, Orff and Kodaly. *British Journal of Music Education*, 26(2), 213–224. doi:10.1017/s0265051709008444.

Bradley, D. (2015). Hidden in plain sight. In C. Benedict, P. Schmidt, G. Spruce, & P. Woodford (Eds.), *The Oxford handbook of social justice in music education* (pp. 190–203). Oxford University Press. doi:10.1093/oxfordhb/9780199356157.001.0001.

Bucholtz, M., Casillas, D. I., & Lee, J. S. (2017). Language and culture as sustenance. In D. Paris & H. S. Alim (Eds.), *Culturally sustaining pedagogies: Teaching and learning for justice in a changing world* (pp. 43–59). Teachers College Press.

Calderon, D. (2011). Locating the foundations of epistemologies of ignorance in education ideology and practice. In E. Malewski & N. Jaramillo (Eds.), *Epistemologies of ignorance in education* (pp. 105–127). Information Age Publishing.

Choate, R. A., Fowler, C. B., Brown, C. E., & Wersen, L. G. (1967). The Tanglewood symposium: Music in American society. *Music Educators Journal*, 54(3), 49–80. doi:10.2307/3391187.

Domínguez, M. (2017). "Se hace puentes al andar:" Decolonial teacher education as a needed bridge to culturally sustaining and revitalizing pedagogies. In D. Paris & H. S. Alim (Eds.), *Culturally sustaining pedagogies: Teaching and learning for justice in a changing world* (pp. 225–245). Teachers College Press.

Eidsheim, N. S. (2019). *The race of sound: Listening, timbre, and vocality in African American music* (p. 288). Duke University Press. doi:10.1215/9781478090359.

Fitzpatrick, K. R. (2012). Cultural diversity and the formation of identity: Our role as music teachers. *Music Educators Journal*, 98(4), 53–59. doi:10.1177/0027432112442903.

Gay, G. (2002). Preparing for culturally responsive teaching. *Journal of Teacher Education*, 53(2), 106–116. doi:10.1177/0022487102053002003.

Gay, G. (2010). *Culturally responsive teaching: Theory, research, and practice* (2nd ed.). Teachers College Press.

González, N., Moll, L. C., & Amanti, C. (Eds.). (2005). *Funds of knowledge: Theorizing practices in households, communities, and classrooms*. Routledge. doi:10.4324/9781410613462.

Gould, E. (2012). Uprooting music education pedagogies and curricula: Becoming-musician and the Deleuzian refrain. *Discourse: Studies in the Cultural Politics of Education*, 33(1), 75–86. doi:10.1080/01596306.2012.632168.

Gustafson, R. I. (2009). *Race and curriculum*. Palgrave MacMillan.

Ladson-Billings, G. (2014). Culturally relevant pedagogy 2.0: A.k.a. the remix. *Harvard Educational Review*, 84(1), 74–84. doi:10.17763/haer.84.1.p2rj131485484751.

Lee, C. D. (2017). An ecological framework for enacting culturally sustaining pedagogy. In D. Paris & H. S. Alim (Eds.), *Culturally sustaining pedagogies: Teaching and learning for justice in a changing world* (pp. 261–273). Teachers College Press.

Lind, V. R., & McKoy, C. L. (2016). *Culturally responsive teaching in music education: From understanding to application*. Routledge. doi:10.4324/9781315747279.

Malewski, E., & Jaramillo, N. (2011). *Epistemologies of ignorance in education*. Information Age Publishing.

## 22 Culturally Sustaining Pedagogy

Morrison, T. (1998, March). From an interview on Charlie Rose. Public Broadcasting Service. Retrieved from http://www.youtube.com/watch?v=F4vIGvKpT1c.

Paris, D. (2012). Culturally sustaining pedagogy: A needed change in stance, terminology, and practice. *Educational Researcher*, 41(3), 93–97. doi:10.3102/0013189x12441244.

Paris, D. (2015). The right to culturally sustaining language education for the new American mainstream: An introduction. *International Multilingual Research Journal*, 9(4), 221–226. doi:10.1080/19313152.2015.1092849.

Paris, D. (2019). Naming beyond the white settler colonial gaze in educational research. *International Journal of Qualitative Studies in Education*, 32(3), 217–224. doi:10.1080/09518398.2019.1576943.

Paris, D., & Alim, H. S. (Eds.). (2017). *Culturally sustaining pedagogies: Teaching and learning for justice in a changing world*. Teachers College Press.

Paris, D., & Alim, H. S. (2014). What are we seeking to sustain through culturally sustaining pedagogy? A loving critique forward. *Harvard Educational Review*, 84(1), 85–100. doi:10.17763/haer.84.1.982l873k2ht16m77.

Rosa, J., & Flores, N. (2017). Do you hear what I hear? Raciolinguistic ideologies and culturally sustaining pedagogies. In D. Paris & H. S. Alim (Eds.), *Culturally sustaining pedagogies: Teaching and learning for justice in a changing world* (pp. 175–190). Teachers College Press.

Shaw, J. T. (2014). *The music I was meant to sing: Adolescent choral students' perceptions of culturally responsive pedagogy* (Doctoral dissertation). Retrieved from ProQuest LLC (UMI No. 3627141).

Shaw, J. T. (2019). *Culturally responsive choral music education: What teachers can learn from nine students' experiences in three choirs*. Routledge. doi:10.4324/9780429503900.

Sleeter, C. E. (2018). Multicultural education past, present, and future: Struggles for dialog and power-sharing. *International Journal of Multicultural Education*, 20(1), 5–20. doi:10.18251/ijme.v20i1.1663.

Stoever, J. L. (2016). *The sonic color line: Race and the cultural politics of listening*. New York University Press. doi:10.2307/j.ctt1bj4s55.

Part II

# Historical Overview of Today's Music Classroom

# 3 Music and the "Civilizing" Mission

## How Did We Get Here?

To enact culturally sustaining music pedagogy, normalized assumptions and practices which perpetuate inequality within the field of music education must first be dismantled, interrogated, and then reimagined. The uncovering of harmful practices, however, is not possible without a reckoning of the ways in which these practices came to be. An historical analysis allows us to trace the origins of contemporary practices and belief systems—the contexts in which these practices were developed and their justifications. Without an historical understanding of contemporary music teaching discourses and their ideological underpinnings, our efforts to expand and equitize music education will fall short. It is in the unearthing of the roots of our practices that we can recognize their contemporary manifestations.

The purpose of the historical research in Part II of this book is to excavate the practices and ideologies which have reified a Western classical musical hegemony throughout North America, Europe, Britain, and the former British colonies. In addition, an historical analysis provides a means by which to better understand, interpret, and situate the student and teacher accounts in Part III. To do so, I examined and analyzed a wide range of documents, policies, and institutional strategies from the nineteenth century to the present. These various sources revealed a trail of hegemony that has attempted to efface the music-making and invisibilize the music-making bodies of minoritized peoples throughout the world.

What is essentially being traced via the examination of documents and policies of the period in question is the insertion of Western, primarily European, elements of music pedagogy, hierarchies of aesthetic value, and most of all the disciplining of music-making bodies. Readers may recognize some of the more prominent names, such as John Curwen, Lowell Mason, and Walter Damrosch, who are still associated with music teaching methods and practices in the United States, Britain, and beyond, but there are many more figures, lost to the popular memory, who established music teaching ideologies and pedagogies that remain embedded in contemporary music teaching practice and contribute to perpetuated exclusion within the field of music education.

DOI: 10.4324/9781003099475-5

## 26  Historical Overview

Historically, Western classical music was not simply another cultural choice among many but instead functioned as a complete displacer of musics variously called "savage" or "primitive." In my historical research, I drew inspiration from the critical work of scholars who have questioned and continue to question dominant historical narratives. One such scholar, for example, Roxanne Dunbar-Ortiz (2014), in her "writing [of] US history from an Indigenous peoples' perspective," has interrogated the historical master narrative which was founded on "settler colonialism and genocide" (p. 2). This narrative, she concludes, is perpetuated because of "an absence of motivation to ask questions that challenge the core of the scripted narrative of the origin story" (p. 2). Dunbar-Ortiz's observation is particularly salient for the field of music education. Why have we not done more to challenge the master narrative of Western classical musical superiority in teaching? My hypothesis is that an *ahistorical* understanding of contemporary Western classical music teaching practices and ideology has allowed for an "unknowing" of their harmful histories, thus deeming an interrogation of them unnecessary. It was because of this hypothesis that I sought an historical understanding of music teaching practices from the perspective of those who have been historically silenced by them.

Calderon (2011), in her discussion about epistemologies of ignorance, asserts that we cannot begin to grapple with the ways in which educational practices and methods have silenced and erased non-Western epistemologies without an historical examination that "trace[s] the origins of theories/methods/methodologies to their originary worldviews. Without doing this, theories/methods/methodologies remain blind to their colonial ontologies" (p. 108). By discovering the ways in which music teaching practices are rooted in coloniality, we can uncover and dismantle the systemic racism embedded in normalized discourses and assumptions. For, as Coates (2014) and Love (2019) remind us, systemic change is impossible with "an ahistorical understanding of oppression" (Love, 2019, p. 92). "An ahistorical understanding" of music teaching methods leads to the uncritical application of those methods without an understanding of the ways in which the methods were used to subvert, coerce, and silence individuals. Coates (2014) describes this as an "à la carte" understanding of historical oppression. He says, "to proudly claim the veteran and disown the slaveholder is patriotism à la carte" (Coates, 2014). In what ways do contemporary music practices perpetuate an "à la carte" history of music education? How does this contribute to exclusion within the field of music education?

The following historical analysis connects contemporary music teaching practices and discourses to their historical and ideological origins. By placing common teaching practices and beliefs within their original context, we can begin to interrogate the ways in which they are presumed to be neutral and superior. An historical analysis dismantles and demystifies standards and methods that have been touted as ahistorical and universally applicable, thus challenging the uncritical reverence of those methods. By demystifying

_Music and the "Civilizing" Mission_  27

that which has come to be accepted as musical truths, the act of questioning and rethinking status quo music teaching assumptions becomes more feasible and less taboo. Most importantly, by shedding light on the ways in which normalized assumptions and pedagogy are tied to colonialist and racist music teaching practices, my hope is that an historical analysis will provide an impetus for pedagogical change.

## Music and "Civilizing"

Throughout history, music education has been used as a means by which to "civilize," "discipline," "convert," and "tame" the "savage," "heathen," and "uncivilized" subject (Olwage, 2005), leading to cultural genocide and hegemony. To justify their actions, the oppressors used discourses of saviorism, betterment, and refinement.

In North America, Western music colonialism was used as a means by which to convert indigenous people to Christianity and in doing so exert control over "land and resources" (Grande, 2015, p. 23). In modern-day Canada, French Jesuits used music as a means by which to coerce Indigenous people. According to Britton (1958), in his historical critique of the beginnings of music education in North America, "Jesuit priests from France habitually depended upon music and delight which the Indians took in it for aid in their missionary endeavors. The _Jesuit Relations_ are full of accounts describing the effects European music exerted upon the Indians" (p. 198).

The Spanish Franciscan Catholic missions in modern-day Mexico and the Southwest region of the United States are credited with the beginnings of European music education in the United States (Spell, 1922). In her account of the man who is credited as the first teacher of European music in America—Pedro de Gante in 1523—Spell (1922) describes how music was "found to exert a remarkable influence over the Indians" (p. 1), and "it was fortunate that the man who began the work of conversion saw fit to utilize the instinct for music" (pp. 5–6). To Spell, de Gante's musical conquest could be likened to that of a musical hero because he and his colleagues imparted "superior" Western classical musical knowledge to those who were "uncivilized." Spell describes the musical mission of de Gante and his colleagues as one of musical saviorism of historical importance in which they "[won] the hearts and elevate[ed] the minds" (p. 3) of the Indigenous people. In addition to "elevated" minds and hearts, Spell credits de Gante for imparting a "love of music" to the colonized, which she reminds the reader, "is a distinguishing characteristic of the Mexican to-day" (Spell, 1922, p. 7).

Spell's (1922) account of de Gante illustrates the ways in which musical colonialism was justified as a means of "enlightening" the colonized. After pillaging and attempting to replace the Indigenous musical traditions of the colonized, the colonizer then was congratulated and credited for also imparting a love of music to them. The assumption was that there had been no musical appreciation prior to de Gante's influence. The belief system with which Spell (1922) articulates the "musical conquest" of de Gante

## 28   Historical Overview

permeated much of colonialist thinking of that time. Music fueled the colonial mission of Christianity and Euro-elitism, conquest and cultural genocide. Although de Gante's cultural mission took place in 1523, the celebration of his musical conquest by Spell in 1922 is telling of the ways in which musical saviorism and musical elitism continued to be celebrated into the twentieth century and remain embedded in contemporary thought.

In the 1958 publication entitled *Basic Concepts in Music Education*, written by members of the Music Educators National Conference and submitted to the National Society for the Study of Education, Britton (1958) articulates the discourses on which American music education was founded. "It is particularly noteworthy that from the very beginning music education in the United States was conditioned by a deliberate desire on the part of cultural leaders to suppress indigenous music and to substitute something 'better' in its place" (p. 200). In his discussion about the history of music education in the United States, Britton notes that "American music and music education are derived directly from the culture of the English colonists" (p. 199). British musical colonialism to which Britton refers, and on which American music education was founded, was rampant in British colonial missions both abroad and at home (Olwage, 2005). Musical moralism—the belief that music has the power to impact a person's morality—was used to justify music education systems of instruction and assessment.

## Britain

John Hullah, well known for his singing school classes at Exeter Hall and his *fixed-doh* sight-singing approach, championed his pedagogical system as a means to "improve" the poor, working class (Olwage, 2005; Rainbow & McGuire, 2014). In her biographical account of her husband, Frances Hullah (1886), John Hullah's second wife, described him as "a firm believer in the softening and civilising influences of his art" (p. 27). She also called him a "reformer," who, with "zeal," strove to "civilize" England's "working and leisured classes" with music (p. 27). According to his wife, Hullah hoped that "England's future condition" would be one in which music had "lulled to rest all savage passions … of the peasant's life" (p. 32). So successful was he in his mission that, as he, according to Frances Hullah, "carried all hearts with him" (p. 32), the press took note of his success in "civilizing" the poor. They "marked Mr. Hullah's efforts with generous appreciation, pointing out the civilising effects of his teaching, as evidenced by the brightening expression and gentler bearing of the members of the poorer singing classes" (p. 62). As an influential figure in the Victorian choralism movement, Hullah, contributed to what Olwage (2005) describes as "disciplining choralism" and "internal colonialism" (p. 28), where choral singing was used as a means by which to control, contain, "civilize," and "save" those who were considered to be "uncivilized." Hullah's impact, therefore, was one in which the poor were coerced to participate in the musical hegemony of internal colonialism.

## Tonic Sol-Fa and the Civilizing Mission

Hullah's music teaching and beliefs about music's "civilizing" potential were succeeded by John Curwen's development of the Tonic Sol-Fa pedagogical system, which he based on Sarah Glover's Sol-Fa approach (Rainbow & McGuire, 2014). Curwen's Tonic Sol-Fa approach, similarly fueled by saviorism, Christianity, and a civilizing rhetoric, grew exponentially within Britain and the colonies. Initially developed in 1841 as a means by which to teach children to sing (Rainbow & McGuire, 2014), so influential was the moral propaganda with which he packaged his music teaching system, that by 1880, Curwen's Tonic Sol-Fa pedagogy had reached "hundreds of thousands of British singers [who] had been trained in the method" (p. 1). It quickly "became the notation of choice for contemporary moral philanthropic movements, such as temperance and missionary organizations" (p. 1).

The Tonic Sol-Fa system was used as a means by which to control and "civilize" the marginalized and the colonized both within Britain proper and as a part of Britain's imperial expansion (Olwage, 2005; 2010). In his discussion about Britain's use of choralism to discipline and contain South Africans during its colonial rule, Olwage (2005) describes a choral performance that took place in Grahamstown, a colonial city in South Africa, in which a Black choir performed Victorian choral repertoire for a White elite audience. The *Grahamstown Journal* review described the concert as an "'unprecedented success'" (p. 26). They attributed the concert's success "to Mr. Curwen's Tonic Sol-Fa system" because, according to the review, Curwen's Tonic Sol-Fa system "'brought the savage within the pale of civilization'" (p. 26). Olwage concludes that the *Grahamstown Journal* reviewer

> was not so much concerned with the choir's performance as with the effect that practices of choir singing had on its black members. In short, the utility of choralism was its civilizing potential, where civilizing ... was synonymous with disciplining.
>
> (Olwage, 2005, p. 26)

The Grahamstown account is emblematic of the ways in which the Tonic Sol-Fa pedagogical system represented much more than just singing and music learning. Rather, because the Victorian musical aesthetics and teaching practices were considered superior and more "civil," the use of them to control and manipulate those for whom these practices were unfamiliar was morally justified or, even worse, deemed morally necessary. As the Tonic Sol-Fa movement grew to an unprecedented reach, the Tonic Sol-Fa leadership sought means by which to further control, rank, and contain those who studied the system. In 1852, they introduced a music certification system with which music students could be tested and ranked (Olwage, 2005). Those who received the certification were placed into elite groups from which the non-certified were excluded. This, as Olwage emphasizes, led to a

## 30 *Historical Overview*

hierarchizing—an explicit exclusion based upon a musical certification with implicit ties to social class and race—as was seen in the colonies. The certificate "functioned as a penalizing exclusion not only of the uncertificated, but of those members of the working classes who had not internalized the message of social betterment through self-improvement" (Olwage, 2005, p. 30). The Tonic Sol-Fa music certification system grew to include certification levels ranging from elementary and intermediate to advanced. Thus, the hierarchizing system of control was further hierarchized. Music certification was used as a means by which to justify musical colonialism and a hegemonic relationship between the music teacher/adjudicator/colonizer and the student/subject/colonized.

Tonic Sol-Fa music teachers and adjudicators who spread the system throughout the British empire found themselves in considerable positions of power. The imposition of a Western classical musical pedagogy and ranking system throughout "Africa, Asia, Australasia, and the Americas" (Rainbow & McGuire, 2014, p. 3) contributed to a widespread, hegemonic music colonialism and musical genocide. So pervasive was the system that, by the twentieth century, "a sixth of all black pupils at African's largest mission institution, Lovedale, in the eastern Cape, were being examined for and awarded sol-fa certificates" (Olwage, 2005, p. 31). The successful expansion of the Tonic Sol-Fa music pedagogy and certification system continued well beyond John Curwen's death in 1880 under the leadership of his son, John Spencer Curwen (Rainbow & McGuire, 2014). "In the 'civilizing mission' at home and in the colonies," (Olwage, 2010, p. 196), Christian and musical conversion were conflated. In fact, so intertwined were they that the Tonic Sol-Fa pedagogical system "became the only notation used or promoted by missionaries" (Rainbow & McGuire, 2014, p. 3).

Not only was the Tonic Sol-Fa pedagogical system used by missionaries, but Tonic Sol-Fa music teachers, themselves, were considered musical missionaries. Much like their contemporary Christian missionaries, the Tonic Sol-Fa teachers were encouraged—as explained in an 1862 article in the *Tonic Sol-Fa Reporter*—to "'sow the seed' of sol-fa in their 'missionary labours'" ("Sol-fa Missions," 1862, p. 326, as cited in Olwage, 2010, p. 196) thus contributing to the imperialist, "civilizing," and "saviorist" rhetoric with which the two were steeped. John Spencer Curwen, himself, noted in his address to the Curwen Club, members of which were "certified Tonic Sol-Faists," that they were "not only musicians but musical missionaries" (Jubilee reports: Jubilation of the Curwen Club, 1891, p. 233). During the same meeting, Reverend Drury, the principal of the Church Missionary College, spoke about the influence of the Tonic Sol-Fa "mission." "The whole tendency of the system ha[s] been towards elevating and purifying, and all that made for the righteousness of the nation" (p. 233). He jokingly spoke about an exchange he had with Mr. Rae, the secretary of the National Temperance League, in which Mr. Rae had

*Music and the "Civilizing" Mission*   31

said that the temperance cause ought to be married to the Tonic Sol - fa system, but, said Mr. Drury, that would be a case of bigamy, because the foreign missionary cause was married to Tonic Sol - fa already.

(p. 233)

The members responded with laughter to Reverend Drury's account demonstrating the ways in which Tonic Sol-Fa was an accepted and sought after means by which to control and subvert the "undisciplined," so much so that Mr. Drury described how he "pictured a party of natives watching a magic lantern screen stretched under a tree, each picture being introduced by native airs, and Christian hymns learnt through Sol-fa" (p. 233). Tonic Sol-Fa, therefore, had become indispensable for Christian and colonialist missions in their efforts to convert, both musically and religiously, the colonized.

These missions contributed to the vast expansion of the Tonic Sol-Fa musical system throughout Britain and the colonies. To celebrate the extensive influence of the Tonic Sol-Fa system throughout the world, in 1891, the Tonic Sol-Fa Association held a Jubilee. This event was attended by people from all over the world. The celebration included a religious service at St. Paul's Cathedral and a "pilgrimage" to John Curwen's grave (Jubilee reports: At the grave of John Curwen, 1891, p. 231), emblematic of the religiosity of the society and Curwen's disciple-worthy stature. The account from the *Musical Herald*, the newly branded *Tonic Sol-Fa Reporter*, in 1891 described the Jubilee as an event in which "thousands of hearts full of thankfulness for the good that Tonic Sol - fa had done" (Jubilee reports: Jubilee service at St. Paul's, 1891, p. 230) were present. Three hundred musicians and visitors took part in the pilgrimage to John Curwen's grave. The sentiments expressed illuminated the ideological underpinnings and saviorist propaganda of the Tonic Sol-Fa musical movement. The first to speak, Reverend Knaggs of Stratford, said that "John Curwen entered into the ministry of music because he saw that there was in it a cheering, elevating, and humanising element ... To him his music mission was as really religious as his mission to preach the Gospel" (p. 231). The account in the *Music Herald* goes on to describe Reverend Knaggs' observations of Curwen's influence in South Africa:

When [he] was in South Africa a few months ago, he found that Curwen's system of music was taught in all the mission stations. The Kaffirs and Zulus easily and readily learnt it ... He thanked God because the system was being made so useful among the coloured people of Africa.

(pp. 231–232)

Both accounts demonstrate the ways in which the Tonic Sol-Fa music pedagogy was conflated with religious saviorism thus becoming musical saviorism, where the music traditions of the colonized, here the Kaffirs and Zulus, were replaced with Western classical music and notation. Much like

## 32 *Historical Overview*

Christian conversion during this time, musical conversion was presumed to be in the best interest of those being converted—their musical cultures being deemed inconsequential in the process.

Other accounts by Jubilee celebration attendees included the speeches of several music educators visiting from the United States. They spoke about the far-reaching influence of the Tonic Sol-Fa movement. Most notable were the ways in which they harnessed expressions of unity among Tonic Sol-Faists in the United States and Britain to accomplish a mutual goal of musical and cultural domination. Mr. Seward, described by Dr. S. McBurney of the *Musical Herald* as "the most enthusiastic advocate of Tonic Sol - fa in the United States" (McBurney 1891, p. 36), gave a rousing speech at Exeter Hall during Jubilee week. According to the *Musical Herald*'s account of his speech:

> He thought all would agree that the one thing which should be true of the English and the American nation was that their hearts should beat as one (applause), and they would also agree that Tonic Sol - fa would help to that grand result (applause), and that among the greatest and most gratifying and most glorious works that they two should be able to accomplish was that of making the whole world musical (loud applause).
> (Jubilee reports: Exeter Hall speeches and singing, 1891, p. 239)

In a similar tone, Dr. Perkins, a music educator and performer from New York, wrote about his impressions of the Jubilee celebration in a letter of congratulations to the President of the Tonic Sol-Fa College. "Any system or method that can accomplish such results as I witnessed last Saturday, whether Sol-fa, Chevé, Chinese, or Choctaw, deserves all the praise that can be bestowed upon it." He went on to encourage them in their mission, which he described as a mission "to extend a knowledge of the art divine among the people, and to elevate them by the refining and humanising influence of the noblest of the arts" (Perkins, 1891, p. 261).

Perkins' and Seward's accounts are representative of the ideology to which the Tonic Sol-Fa's success can be attributed. The music pedagogy, based on Western classical musical notation and aesthetics, was believed to be universally appropriate for all contexts. In addition to being universal, the pedagogy was considered to be superior, thereby justifying its imposition on colonized peoples with vastly different heritages. The ideological crux, however, was the assumption that this music pedagogy would "civilize," "humanize," "refine," and "elevate" those to whom it was introduced. Perkins and Seward both congratulated the Tonic Sol-Fa imperial mission and suggested that it was a mutual endeavor to make "the whole world musical" (Jubilee reports: Exeter Hall speeches and singing, 1891, p. 239)—a mission that lent itself well to the American expansion upon peoples and cultures under the auspices of "betterment," "saviorism," and "manifest destiny."

## Tonic Sol-Fa and Western Classical Vocal Pedagogy

Perhaps the most crucial aspect of the Tonic Sol-Fa method and its lasting impact on contemporary music education worldwide was its intertwining of vocal pedagogy with sight-singing teaching. Modern vocal pedagogy championed by Garcia in his 1847 treatise, *Traité Complet de L'art du Chant*, based on scientific advances in vocal science and acoustics, marked the advent of the singing subject, disciplined and controlled by the singing teacher. Classical vocal technique and the pedagogy with which it is associated became the "scientifically proven correct" and "healthy" way to sing allowing for a hierarchizing of singing and a ranking of singing subjects based upon "scientific principles." The acoustic principles on which classical vocal technique was based stipulated the ways in which the vocal tract could be manipulated to change the sound. Garcia championed the lowering of the larynx in particular as a means by which to achieve the "ideal" sound (Stark, 2003, p. 37). This ideal sound, however, was for a specific context and setting, namely the operatic stage. In his work with the laryngoscope, which he perfected in 1854 (Potter, 2006, p. 55), Garcia sought to better understand vocal anatomy so that he might perfect his operatic singing and teaching. It was in the delineation of vocal ideals for operatic singing that he determined the ideal laryngeal position and glottal closure.

Although Garcia never claimed to be championing a universal singing ideal, his operatic ideals became the vocal standards of vocal pedagogy reaching music educators throughout Europe, the United States, and Britain's colonies. The ideology in which this pedagogy was entangled, namely operatic ideals, formed the basis of "correct" singing for generations to come. Vocal teaching became a means with which music educators could manipulate, homogenize, and discipline their students' voices. For a disciplining musical movement like Curwen's Tonic Sol-Fa movement, Garcia's vocal pedagogy and vocal standards provided the ideal means by which to rank and hierarchize bodies and voices.

In his *Standard Course of Lessons and Exercises in the Tonic Sol-fa Method of Teaching Music* manual, Curwen's (1872) opening section is dedicated to the "Tonic Sol-Fa Method of Teaching to Sing" (p. 1). Drawing from Garcia's ideals, he describes a "proper" singing tone, "proper" singing posture, and "proper" breath management for singing. His explicit instructions, drawn from Garcia's treatise, require that the singing subject exhibit control and discipline over his singing body. "Proper," therefore, is synonymous with contrived. A singer must, therefore, act against his natural tendencies to achieve this technique, which is noted by Curwen (1872). "These rules have to be carefully studied by the singer, and, at first, they will make him stiff and self-conscious; but soon, and with care, the proper position will *grow into a habit*" (p. 2, original emphasis).

By positioning a singer against his natural inclinations, vocal teaching would require a master to discipline and oversee a singer's progress.

34  *Historical Overview*

According to Curwen (1872), "The teacher 'calls his pupils into position' by giving out as words of command ... at each order, the pupils take the position ... and the teacher watches to make sure that they do so properly" (p. 2). Curwen's instructions, militaristic in tone, required a disciplining of singers' bodies from their lips to their feet:

> The singer should *(a)* *stand* with heels together or in the soldiers posture of "stand at ease;" *(b)* with *head* erect, but not thrown back; *(c)* with shoulders held back, but not up; *(d)* with lungs kept naturally filled—not with raised chest, except on extraordinary occasions—but with the ribs, never allowed to collapse, pressing against the clothes at each side, and the lower muscles of the abdomen drawn in; *(e)* with the mouth freely open, but not in the fish-mouth shape O,—the lips being pressed upon the teeth, and drawn somewhat away from the opening, so as not to deaden the sound,—the lower jaw falling,—the palate so raised as to *catch* on its front-part the stream of air from the lungs,—and the tongue flat, its tip just touching the lower teeth.
>
> (Curwen, 1872, p. 2)

Vocal pedagogy provided a means of control and discipline for both the teacher and student. Discipline within the Tonic Sol-Fa movement and Victorian Britain was conflated with morality and elitism. Curwen's interpretation of Garcia's treatise, therefore, lent itself well to the savioristic mission of the Tonic Sol-Fa movement. According to Curwen, vocal discipline was necessary for the teaching of Tonic Sol-Fa because, as he states in his singing manual, "There is no other way in which the pupil can be saved from slovenly habits and coarse flat singing" (p. 3).

Vocal pedagogy was an effective means by which to exert further control over Tonic Sol-Fa students in the effort to "save" and "improve" them. In this sense, morality, elitism, discipline, class improvement, and control were intertwined as a means by which to subvert those who were "in need of refinement" to a hegemonic destruction of their own vocal agency. Vocal homogenization, standardization, and purification became the discourses of justification for vocal hegemony. Beginning singers were only permitted to sing "softly" (Curwen, 1872, p. 2) to ensure they developed "correct" habits. This softening or silencing of a student's voice reinforced the belief that students should be self-conscious and inhibited in their vocal production. Curwen (1872) uses specific language to describe a "correct" and "incorrect" singing voice, suggesting that vocal timbre aesthetics can be objectively judged based upon pre-conceived criteria. By quoting the vocal pedagogue Emma Seiler, Curwen juxtaposes a "correct" and "incorrect" sound and the work voice teachers must do "'to form' says Madame Seiler, 'out of a sharp, hard, and disagreeable voice, a voice sweet and pleasing'" (pp. 1–2).

A binary between a "good" and "bad" voice gave teachers the power to determine whose voices were acceptable. This distinguishing of good and bad vocality extended into society at-large. Vocal quality became a means by which to distinguish the disciplined elite who had been vocally trained from the untrained. As Potter so aptly describes it,

> It is only in the nineteenth century that the artistic use of the voice acquired the technique which would finally separate it completely from every other way of singing ... a music that was for the elite of society required a technique that was for its exclusive use.
>
> (Potter, 2006, pp. 63–64)

The combination of Curwen's Tonic Sol-Fa movement with Garcia's vocal pedagogy provided the means by which to teach, discipline, and control under the guise of musical and class refinement. Garcia's technique for operatic singing became the vocal "standard" for music education settings, narrowly defining the vocal aesthetics to which music educators would aspire for generations to come. The detriment of this "standardization" continues to be felt in music education settings worldwide.

### Tonic Sol-Fa, Precursor for the ABRSM Music Certification System

Although the Tonic Sol-Fa movement in its original form ceases to exist today, remnants of its influence remain intact within music teaching and learning settings worldwide (Rainbow & McGuire, 2014, p. 5). The Tonic Sol-Fa certification system and the ways in which that system ranked and disseminated musical "standards" were adopted by the Royal College of Music and the Royal Academy of Music in 1889 (Wright, 2013). In a combined effort, the two organizations became the Associated Board of the Royal Schools of Music— known by 2012 as ABRSM—with its own musical examination system. Much like the Tonic Sol-Fa system, the impetus for the ABRSM system was to "elevate" the musical standards and to promote "the cultivation of music as an art" (Wright, 2013, p. 76) throughout the British empire. The musical art and "standards" being promoted were from the Western classical music tradition and fueled by the same elitist, saviorist rhetoric with which the Tonic Sol-Fa music examination system was entangled. According to the ABRSM historian, "in the course of its 120 years few institutions can be said to have had a greater effect on people's musical lives across the world" (Wright, 2013, p. 1), thus alluding to the discourses of "betterment" and "improvement" on which the musical examination system was built. Again, the "great effect" to which he refers was in opposition to local musical cultures.

In his historical account of the ABRSM music examination system, Wright (2013) emphasizes the ways in which the system of assessment normalized a particular music education epistemology.

> We see that there are many ways in which music exams determine the cultural expectations of those learning to play or sing ... and a means to

## 36 *Historical Overview*

label standards of attainment. Thus, in a variety of ways, grade exams, as in "doing the grades", have fashioned many people's understanding of what constitutes "normal" practice in music teaching.

(Wright, 2013, p. 3)

The homogenization of a Eurocentric, normalized music education practice spread quickly throughout Britain and its empire allowing for a hierarchization of Western classical music "standards" over local music traditions. By 1948, ABRSM examinations were taking place in South Africa, Australia, New Zealand, Canada, Malta, the West Indies, "India, Pakistan, Ceylon (now Sri Lanka), Malta, Rhodesia (now Zimbabwe), Cyprus, Singapore and Kenya," and "by 1981 ABRSM was examining more than 460,000 candidates a year" (ABRSM, n.d.).

Wright (2013) notes that:

The grade process is a conditioning factor in the musical taste, habits and attitudes of candidates and their teachers ... the syllabuses put out by examination boards have shaped the way that very many teachers teach, and have defined musical standards and musical taste for millions of people.

(Wright, 2013, p. 6)

The musical "standards" and "tastes" pioneered by the ABRSM music examination system have been disseminated through discourses of superiority and elitism. Western classical music "standards" and the popularity of the ABRSM examination system in postcolonial countries have marginalized local music-making and teaching practices. The homogenization of music education based upon a Western classical pedagogical practice has allowed for a ranking and disciplining of musical bodies and musical traditions throughout the world. The contemporary ramifications of this is felt by the "650,000 candidates ... in more than 90 countries" worldwide (ABRSM, n. d.). According to ABRSM, the "new partnerships and innovative new products in the ABRSM pipeline" are indicative of their success and suggest that, in their words, their "future looks—and sounds—as promising as ever" (ABRSM, n.d.). The pipeline to which they are referring is culturally, musically, and epistemologically specific. Despite this specificity, the ABRSM mission is to universalize this particular music teaching practice with little effort to diversify their system. They stipulate that "the marking criteria followed by examiners for graded exams have remained remarkably consistent over the course of ABRSM's history" (ABRSM, n.d.).

The dissemination of Western classical music teaching practices, normalized "standards" and aesthetics through the imperialist, and the "civilizing" missions of the Tonic Sol-Fa and ABRSM musical examination systems have all contributed to a hegemonic power structure of music education throughout the world.

## References

ABRSM. (n.d.) Our history. https://us.abrsm.org/en/about-us/our-history/.

Britton, A. (1958). Music in early American public education: A historical critique. In N. B. Henry (Ed.), *Basic concepts in music education* (pp. 195–211). University of Chicago Press.

Calderon, D. (2011). Locating the foundations of epistemologies of ignorance in education ideology and practice. In E. Malewski & N. Jaramillo (Eds.), *Epistemologies of ignorance in education* (pp. 105–127). Information Age Publishing.

Coates, T. N. (2014, June). The case for reparations. *The Atlantic*, 313(5), 54–71.

Curwen, J. (1872). *The standard course of lessons and exercises in the Tonic Sol-fa method of teaching music*. Tonic Sol-Fa Agency.

Dunbar-Ortiz, R. (2014). *An indigenous peoples' history of the United States*. Beacon Press.

García, M. (1847). *Traité complet de l'art du chant en deux parties*. Heugel.

Grande, S. (2015). *Red pedagogy: Native American social and political thought*. Rowman & Littlefield.

Hullah, F. (1886). *Life of John Hullah, LL. D., by his wife*. Longmans, Green.

Jubilee reports: At the grave of John Curwen. (1891, August 1). *Musical Herald*, 521, 231–233.

Jubilee reports: Exeter Hall speeches and singing. (1891, August 1). *Musical Herald*, 521, 237–239.

Jubilee reports: Jubilation of the Curwen Club. (1891, August 1). *Musical Herald*, 521, 233.

Jubilee reports: Jubilee service at St. Paul's. (1891, August 1). *Musical Herald*, 521, 230–231.

Love, B. L. (2019). *We want to do more than survive: Abolitionist teaching and the pursuit of educational freedom*. Beacon Press.

McBurney, S. (1891, February 1). *Musical Herald*, 515, 35–37.

Olwage, G. (2005). Discipline and choralism: The birth of musical colonialism. In A. J. Randall (Ed.), *Music, power, and politics*, (pp. 25–46). Routledge. doi:10.4324/9780203329757-4.

Olwage, G. (2010). Singing in the Victorian world: Tonic sol-fa and discourses of religion, science and Empire in the Cape Colony. *Muziki* 7(2), 193–215. doi:10.1080/18125980.2010.526801.

Perkins, W. O. (1891, September 1). Dr. Perkins on the Jubilee. *Musical Herald*, 522, 261.

Potter, J. (2006). *Vocal authority: Singing style and ideology*. Cambridge University Press.

Rainbow, B., & McGuire, C. (2014). Tonic sol-fa. *Grove Music Online*. Retrieved December 31, 2020, from https://www-oxfordmusiconline-com.ezproxy.butler.edu/grovemusic/view/10.1093/gmo/9781561592630.001.0001/omo-9781561592630-e-0000028124.

Spell, L. (1922). The first teacher of European music in America. *The Catholic Historical Review*, 8(3), 372–378.

Stark, J. (2003). *Bel canto: A history of vocal pedagogy*. University of Toronto Press.

Wright, D. C. (2013). *The Associated Board of the Royal Schools of Music: A social and cultural history*. Boydell Press.

# 4 Music and the "Civilizing" Mission in the United States

While Britain was using the Tonic Sol-Fa pedagogical system as part of its "civilizing mission" to "civilize" and "elevate" the characters of those in need of "civilizing," across the Atlantic Ocean in the United States, a similar "civilizing mission" had been enacted. This musical mission was part of the American effort to control and "civilize" Native Americans. In her poignant account of the educational history of Native Americans in the United States, Grande (2015) states:

> The miseducation of American Indians precedes the "birth" of this nation. From the time of invasion to the present day, the church and state have acted as coconspirators in the theft of Native America, robbing indigenous peoples of their right to be indigenous.
>
> (p. 15)

With the justification of Christian saviorism and the civilizing of the "uncivilized," using education, the United States sought to replace Native American culture with Western culture. In 1819, the Civilization Fund Act "for the civilization of the Indian tribes" was passed "for the purpose of ... introducing among them the habits and arts of civilization and to employ capable persons of good moral character to instruct them" (Civilization Fund Act, 1819). Tied to the church and morality, the arts were a fundamental tool used in the educational colonization of Native Americans and the White saviorist attempt to erase and replace Native American culture. As Grande (2015) attests, "The work of teachers, church leaders, and missionaries were hardly distinguishable during this era; saving souls and colonizing minds became part and parcel of the same colonialist project" (p. 16).

The Indian Removal Act of 1830 and the brutal "forced march of the Cherokee Nation" in 1838 (Dunbar-Ortiz, 2014, p. 112) led to the displacement of 70,000 Native Americans (pp. 110–111) from their land and the brutal deaths of half of the Cherokee, Muskogee, and Seminole populations and 15 percent of the Chickasaws and Choctaws populations (p. 113). In the wake of displacement, death, and violence, the newly created Office of Indian Affairs was tasked to, among other things, "civilize" and educate

DOI: 10.4324/9781003099475-6

## Music and the "Civilizing" Mission in the US   39

Native Americans. "In the following decades the church and state conspired in the development of a variety of 'manual labor schools'" which included "forced labor as part of Indian education" (Grande, 2015, p. 17). The manual labor day schools then were abandoned in favor of manual labor boarding schools towards the end of the nineteenth century. The boarding school setting was considered a more effective means by which to "civilize" Native American children and replace their culture and belief systems with White European, Christian culture and beliefs.

Captain Richard Henry Pratt, one of the first to champion the boarding school as an effective means by which to "civilize" Native American children and the founder of the first Indian boarding school, The Carlisle Indian School (1879–1918), made his claim in an 1892 conference address entitled: "The Advantages of Mingling Indians with Whites" (Pratt, 1892, pp. 46–59). In his address, which was filled with White supremacist, saviorist, and racist rhetoric towards Native Americans and African Americans, Pratt argued that the "Indian problem" could be solved by "kill[ing] the Indian in him, and sav[ing] the man" (Pratt, 1892, p. 46). This belief was part of the ideological underpinnings of his "civilizing" mission at the government-funded Carlisle Indian School. To support his claim, Pratt argued that the impact of slavery on African Americans was a positive one. Slavery, according to Pratt, saved African Americans from their "savage" origins and was "the greatest blessing that ever came to the Negro race—seven millions of blacks from cannibalism in darkest Africa to citizenship in free and enlightened America" (Pratt, 1892, p. 51).

As a result of slavery, Pratt suggested, African Americans were "blessed" to be "forced into association with English-speaking and civilized people," because they too "became English-speaking and civilized." Had slavery not taken place, African Americans, according to Pratt, would have been "Left in Africa, surrounded by their fellow-savages" and "would still be savages" (Pratt, 1892, p. 51). It was with this description of the ways in which Pratt believed slavery had "saved" and "civilized" the African "savages," that Pratt argued for the same approach to "civilize" Native Americans. "Transfer the savage-born infant to the surroundings of civilization, and he will grow to possess a civilized language and habit" (p. 56). Immersion into White, "civilized" society, therefore, Pratt argued, was the only way in which to erase and replace Native American culture.

With this White supremacist ideology and White saviorist propaganda, Pratt opened the first of many Native American boarding schools in the United States. The physical abuse and attempts to "civilize" and erase Native American children's cultures through force, intimidation, and fear are well documented (Grande, 2015; Dunbar-Ortiz, 2014; Embree, 1939; McBeth, 1983; Nabokov, 1999; Smith, 2001). According to Dunbar-Ortiz,

> The experience of generations of Native Americans in on- and off-reservation boarding schools, run by the federal government or Christian missions,

contributed significantly to the family and social dysfunction still found in Native communities. Generations of child abuse, including sexual abuse—from the founding of the first schools by missionaries in the 1830s and the federal government in 1875 until most were closed and the remaining ones reformed in the 1970s—traumatized survivors and their progeny.

(Dunbar-Ortiz, 2014, pp. 211–212)

## Carlisle Indian Boarding School

Upon arriving at the boarding school, Native American children were stripped of their clothing, forced to adopt Christian names, and "their long hair was clipped to the skull" (Nabokov, 1999, p. 216), all of which was a deliberate means on the part of the school to symbolize the eradication of the children's cultures. The Carlisle Indian Boarding school and others documented the "transformation" of the Native American "savages" as a means by which to demonstrate their effective "civilizing" mission.

In his documentation of Native American testimony, Nabokov (1999) shares the stories of Native American children who experienced boarding school. Lone Wolf from the Blackfeet Nation describes the day in which he was taken from his family, at age eight, to attend a boarding school.

*Figure 4.1* White Buffalo, Cheyenne Nation, 1881 (left); White Buffalo, 1882 (right).
Source: Photos courtesy of Carlisle Indian School Digital Resource Center.

*Music and the "Civilizing" Mission in the US* 41

*Figure 4.2* Tom Torlino, Navajo Nation, 1882 (left); Tom Torlino, 1885 (right).
*Source*: Photos courtesy of Carlisle Indian School Digital Resource Center.

Oh, we cried for this was the first time we were to be separated from our parents. I remember looking back at Na-tah-ki and she was crying too .... Once there, our belongings were taken from us, even the little medicine bags our mothers had given us to protect us from harm. Everything was placed in a heap and set afire. Next was the long hair, the pride of all the Indians. The boys one by one would break down and cry when they saw their braids thrown on the floor. All of the buckskin clothes had to go and we had to put on the clothes of the White Man .... We were told never to talk Indian and if we were caught, we got a strapping with a leather belt.

(Nabokov, 1999, p. 220)

In addition to physical harm, psychological and cultural brainwashing took place at the boarding schools. At the Carlisle Boarding School, Sun Elk recounted such trauma:

They told us that Indian ways were bad. They said we must get civilized. I remember that word too. It means "be like the white man." I am willing to be like the white man, but I did not believe Indian ways were wrong. But they kept teaching us for seven years. And the books told how bad Indians had been to the white men—burning their towns and killing their women and children. But I had seen white men do that to Indians. We all wore white man's clothes and ate white man's food and went to white man's churches and spoke white man's talk. And so after a while we also began to say Indians were bad. We laughed at our own people and their blankets and cooking pots and sacred societies and dances.

(Nabokov, 1999, p. 222)

The militaristic and violent means by which students at the Carlisle Indian School were forced to abandon their cultural ways of being, and adopt White European culture, left them no choice but to do so or face violent repercussions. Curriculum at the Carlisle School included Western classical musical training. According to a 1902 catalog, students learned "tone and breathing exercises, breath control, staff notation, analysis, and choral works in four parts" (Catalogue of the Indian industrial school, 1902). In addition, many of them participated in the Carlisle Indian School's band and choir. The band and choir provided Pratt with the means by which to publicly showcase the ways in which he had successfully "civilized" and "encultured" the Native American students. Classical vocal teaching and the militaristic marching band allowed for the disciplining and controlling of students' bodies and voices.

In 1894, the Carlisle band and choir toured "Washington, Baltimore, Wilmington, Philadelphia, New York, and Brooklyn" (*The Indian Helper*, 1894, p. 1). According to an article written in *The Red Man*, an in-house publication, the purpose of the concert tour was to demonstrate "better systems of educating Indian youth into civilization and useful citizenship, as well as to show that under influences of favorable environment the Indian may also acquire refined musical qualities" (*The Red Man*, 1894, p. 3). "Refined musical qualities," namely Western classical musical training, therefore, were equated with "civilization and useful citizenship." By participating in the Western classical musical performance, making sounds that were "appropriate" within that musical tradition, and dressing "appropriately" for the occasion, the Native American choir and band were subjected to a racialized musical hegemony—one in which their identities and cultures were erased. The concerts provided aural and

*Figure 4.3* Carlisle Indian School Band and Choir.
Source: Photos courtesy of Carlisle Indian School Digital Resource Center.

visible evidence of cultural genocide, which for Pratt and the public were markings of a successful "civilizing" mission.

Numerous newspaper articles described how audiences were surprised by the "discipline" and "whiteness" of the performances—both because of the musical sounds presented and the comportment of the performers. Whiteness was evident in both the disciplining of bodies and the disciplining of sound. An article in the *Wilmington News* said:

> The vocal and instrumental music given by the choir and by the band was something of a revelation to those who were present. We naturally do not associate the Indian with music, as we know it among the whites, but the work which was given last night demonstrates what a musical training can do even for the native American people. It showed that, as William Congreve wrote, "Music has charms to soothe a savage breast".
> (*Wilmington News*, 1894, p. 4)

The *Baltimore Sun* suggested that "if these young Indians did nothing else by their Washington visit they cannot but fail to have impressed every one with their docility, good manners and desire to enjoy what was provided for their pleasure and instruction" (*Baltimore Sun*, 1894, p. 2). So successful was Pratt at white-washing the Native American performers with Western classical "ideals" that the *Wilmington News*, as well as other publications, considered the Carlisle school to be the solution to the "Indian problem" and an effective means by which to ensure cultural genocide.

> The idea of the Indian schools is the practical solution of what has so long been called the Indian problem .... By educating the young as the school at Carlisle and the schools in the West are doing, the Indians will become assimilated more and more among the whites, and in another century—probably before—the Indian as an Indian, and as we know him to-day, will be nothing more than a memory.
> (Wilmington News, 1894, p. 4)

The *Baltimore Sun*'s account of the performance suggested that the answer to the "Indian problem" was not merely the school itself, but the Western classical musical training the students received as a means to "civilize" their natural inclinations.

> If these young people have their minds filled with any dreams of war-whoop and the tomahawk they manage to keep it to themselves. Like the civilized world, their training represents the product of their environment and seem to the authorities of Carlisle school to better answer the problem of Indian development from savage to civilized habits than has been attained in any other way.
> (*Baltimore Sun*, 1894, p. 2)

## 44 *Historical Overview*

In response to the concerts, Western classical musical teaching was touted not only as a means by which to "civilize" the "savage" but also a "gift" bestowed upon the Carlisle students, and according to the *Baltimore Sun*'s account, "the finer impulses which the music itself has stirred in these children of the reservation" (*Baltimore Sun*, 1894, p. 2). Pratt presented the concerts to the public as examples of musical saviorism and musical progress. The *Christian Advocate* described Pratt's musical saviorism as a "philanthropic" endeavor to "civilize" and "Christianize" the Native American musicians (The *Christian Advocate*, as cited in *The Red Man*, 1894, p. 3). Further, The *Christian Advocate* compared Pratt's success to "evolutionary" progress (p. 3), referring to the theory of Social Darwinism, a theory which gained traction in the United States and Britain at the end of the nineteenth century (Volk, 2004). Social Darwinism justified Eurocentric superiority and the ranking of musical knowledge systems. The use of Western classical music teaching to colonize and erase the students' musical cultures was applauded and considered to be part of the "natural selection" evolutionary process. The *Baltimore Sun* described the musical evolution that the Carlisle students' performance embodied:

> The tom-tom has developed into a band of thirty instruments, which will interpret to this cultivated audience, compositions of Wagner, and Paderewski, and do it well. The savage but rhythmical wolf-song has been improved upon, until this chorus of forty voices can sing us with taste, Mozart's "Gloria."
>
> (*Baltimore Sun*, 1894, p. 2)

The Native American students' bodies and voices, considered signifiers of "savagery" to the audiences of 1894, now encapsulated musical and cultural progress. The linchpin for this hegemonic musical spectacle was for the "saved and civilized" performers to attest to being "saved." Pratt orchestrated this with a speech given by one of the students, Elmer Simon, of the Chippewa Nation before the concert, in which he stated:

> We the Band and Choir of the Carlisle Indian Industrial School feel this to be the proudest moment of our lives. It gives to us the great privilege ... before this distinguished audience, the opening day of new and better conditions for our race which has for centuries repelled your civilization .... Your civilization has conquered us, your beneficence is educating and training us, and we have entered the race for the good things of life with you, adopting your dress, learning your language, occupations and refinements .... We do not profess to have reached the highest we are capable of but we are progressing and hope to demonstrate to you that even your music charms and wins us Savages.
>
> (*The Indian Helper*, 1894, p. 4)

Elmer's speech was also celebrated in the *Washington Evening Star* and the *Baltimore Sun*. We have no way of knowing the amount of coercion that took place to get Elmer to say these things, as the publications of the event are all written from the standpoint of the oppressor, all of which suggest that it was an honor imparted upon him. What we do know, however, is that at these concerts, Elmer was positioned, both in body and voice, in front of a White audience as a symbol of the boarding school's cultural and musical conquest. In doing so, Elmer was forced to participate in the destruction of his own musical and cultural self.

## Fisk Jubilee Singers

The use of Western classical vocal technique as a means to "refine" and "discipline" the body and voice for public performance was a common occurrence in the late nineteenth century. A few years before the Carlisle Indian Boarding school's choir and band concert tour, the Fisk Jubilee Singers of Tennessee embarked upon their first choral tour. The Fisk Free Colored School, an African American school, later becoming Fisk University, was established by the American Missionary Association (AMA) in 1866 (Ward, 2000). Missionary teachers from the AMA, with a White, Protestant worship style, sought to convert and educate newly freed slaves at the Fisk School. They believed that education and Christianity would prevent their students from "revert [ing] to the animism of their African forebears" (Ward, 2000, p. 100).

It bears emphasizing that one of the foundational purposes of the Fisk School's establishment was to teach "control" and "discipline" over the emotional nature of African American worship. John Ogden, one of the school's founders, "believed that education was the solution to what he regarded as the dangerous emotionalism of African American worship" (Ward, 2000, p. 105). In an address he gave to teachers entitled "The Bible as an Educator," Ogden suggested:

> give these poor narrow-minded people our education, and they ... will control themselves and their religion too. The reason their religion is all impulse and animal excitement, is because there is nothing but impulse and animal there for it to operate upon.
>
> (as cited in Ward, 2000, p. 105)

Ogden's racist views of the African American worship style were commonly held views amongst White educators and missionaries, both in the South and in the North. At the beginning of the nineteenth century, Black churches in the North sought independence from their White counterparts, oftentimes with resistance from White church leaders. Those who resisted the independence of African American churches did so because they assumed their "moral" obligation "towards the suppression of a growing evil" (Watson, 1819, p. v). This "evil" according to repressive thinkers such as the minister

46  *Historical Overview*

John Watson writing in his book, *Methodist Error*, in 1819, was "the unprofitable emotions of *screaming, hallowing*, and *jumping*, and the *stepping and singing* of senseless, merry airs" (p. v, original emphasis).

In response to this resistance, leaders of the Bethel African Methodist Episcopal (AME) Church, one of whom succeeded in becoming independent, albeit, "after a long court battle," felt it necessary to assuage the fears of the White Methodist church by demonstrating that "the AME Church intended to maintain the high standards of the mother Methodist Church. The 'doctrines and discipline' of the White church were taken over almost intact into the *Doctrines and Discipline of the African American Methodist Episcopal Church*" (Southern, 1977, p. 301). In the introduction to *The African Methodist Pocket Hymn Book* (1818), Richard Allen, Daniel Coker, and James Champion, leaders of the church, urged African American congregants to "retain the spirit of singing" (p. 4) referring to their White sister church's discomfort with animated singing and dancing.

The disciplining of singing bodies was deemed necessary for African American church leaders to convince White church leaders in the North of the religiosity of their congregations. Similarly, in the South, White preachers assumed their presumed "moral" duty to educate African Americans on how to be religious. A White Georgian preacher by the name of Charles Colcock Jones authored a book devoted entirely to *The Religious Instruction of the Negroes in the United States* (1842). According to Jones, "The strictest order should be preserved at all the religious meetings of the Negroes .... No audible expressions of feeling in the way of groanings, cries, or noises of any kind should be allowed" (Jones, 1842, p. 262). In addition, Jones continued, "one great advantage in teaching them good psalms and hymns, is that they are thereby induced to lay aside the extravagant and nonsensical chants and catches and hallelujah songs of their own composing" (p. 266).

It was within this ideological climate, permeated by discourses which equated morality to quiet utterance and staid bodies, that the Fisk Jubilee choir was formed. The founder and director of the choir, George Leonard White, a White missionary from the North, took it upon himself to impart the values of the church in his musical direction. Influenced by the Tonic Sol-Fa movement and Western classical vocal pedagogy, White, apparently "drilled incessantly ... his ear was exquisite .... In rehearsals his indomitable will never rested until the effect he wished was produced" (Ward, 2000, p. 115). White's exposure to the Tonic Sol-Fa method and Western classical vocal technique can be credited to Theodore F. Seward, among others, who was present at the Tonic Sol-Fa Jubilee in Britain and considered by the *Musical Herald* to be "the most enthusiastic advocate of Tonic Sol - fa in the United States" (McBurney, 1891, p. 36). Seward, as editor of the *Tonic Sol-Fa Advocate*, emphasized the religious underpinnings of the musical pedagogy:

*Music and the "Civilizing" Mission in the US* 47

[I]t must be regarded as a humanitarian and religious rather than a strictly musical movement. In England, Tonic-Sol-fa has been identified in all its history with mission schools, temperance work, and with every effort for the elevation of the multitudes.

(Seward, 1882a, p. 145)

Seward proclaimed, "Tonic Sol-Fa is like religion … spread abroad through the whole human race. What a new world of pleasure would be opened, and not only of pleasure, but of refinement, of elevation, of purity" (Seward, 1882b, p. 134).

Seward championed the aims of the Tonic Sol-Fa movement to strive for "purity," "refinement" and morality through music teaching. García's (1847) vocal pedagogy was also paramount for the musical method. In Seward's book, *A Temple Choir*, Lowell Mason authors the section on vocal pedagogy and quotes García in his discussion about a "pure" vocal tone (Seward, 1867, p. 15). Drawing from García, Mason writes, much like Curwen in his section on the "Tonic Sol-Fa Method of Teaching to Sing" (Curwen, 1872, p. 1) about timbre or resonance as "good" or "bad." For Curwen, it is the difference between a "hard wiry voice" and a "soft clear voice" (Curwen, 1872, p. 1). For Mason, a timbre that is not pure is one that is "guttural or nasal" (Seward, 1867, p. 15). Mason states that "resonance is to hearing what odor is to smelling, or flavor to the taste" (Seward, 1867, p. 15) suggesting that tastes, whether they be aural or oral can be universalized and deduced to "good" or "bad." Influenced by Seward and the same vocal ideology as Mason and Curwen, White's rehearsal discipline with the Fisk Jubilee Singers was fueled by his "horror of harsh tones" therefore, "everything was softened" (Ward, 2000, p. 115). In addition, just as Curwen instructed teachers to "make a sign to those who do not keep their teeth about two finger-breadths apart" (Curwen, 1872, p. 2), White instructed his singers "to sing with their mouths open wide enough to fit a finger between their teeth. The singers had to blend with each other" (Ward, 2000, p. 115).

Perhaps, White's adoption of the Western classical singing technique and Tonic Sol-Fa music pedagogy to, what he and the other school officials believed, "save" the African American singers is best articulated by Erastus Milo Cravath, one of the founders of the Fisk School, in his introduction to Seward's (1872) book *Jubilee Songs: As Sung by the Jubilee Singers of Fisk University*:

By the severe discipline to which the Jubilee Singers have been subjected in the school-room, they have been educated out of the peculiarities of the Negro dialect, and they do not attempt to imitate the peculiar pronunciation of their race. They have also received considerable musical instruction, and have become familiar with much of our best sacred and classical music, and this has modified their manner of execution. They do not attempt to imitate the grotesque bodily motions or the drawling

## 48 *Historical Overview*

intonations that often characterize the singing of great congregations of the colored people in their excited religious meetings.

(Seward, 1872, p. 29)

For White, Cravath, and the school leaders, it was imperative that, through disciplined training, the Fisk Jubilee Singers abandon salient aspects of their musical culture and in doing so, their musical identities. Musical embodiment and musical entrainment, which they describe as "grotesque" was replaced with a staid presence. According to Cravath, Western classical music and its accompanying pedagogies "cured" the students of their "peculiarities." The students' voices, both the timbre and the dialect, were replaced with Western classical timbre aesthetics and Dominant American English. In essence, the "civilizing" mission of the Fisk School robbed students of their musical agency and silenced their vocal identities, all of which was done under the auspices of Christian saviorism and moral improvement.

Much like the Carlisle Indian School choir, the Fisk Jubilee Singers' bodies and voices were disciplined and "trained" to achieve a performance that would suit the White audience both on and off stage. On stage, their voices and bodies needed to adhere to Western classical performance aesthetics. Off stage, they were required to, according to Ward, "constantly comport[ing] themselves as pious, scrupulous young Christian ambassadors of their race" (Ward, 2000, p. 186). The reviews of the Fisk Jubilee Singers' performances shed light on the audiences' perceptions of the African American singers' embodiment of Western classical music aesthetics. In their assessment of Black bodies sounding and looking familiar, White audiences, to affirm their "superiority," sought a means by which to exoticize or infantilize the performers. In other words, Black bodies acting "grotesquely" and "strangely" was uncomfortable for White audiences, but Black bodies acting and sounding too familiar was even more unnerving.

The marking of the singers' performance as simultaneously acceptable and strange allowed the White listener to retain a position of power. The language used to describe the Western classical singing was "sweet," "clear," "musical," "natural," "pleasing," "precise," and equated to "culture," "artistic class," and "high order." This language was countered with descriptions of what the listener considered "strange," "weird," "quaint," "peculiar," and "wild" (*American Missionary Supplement*, 1872). One such review which juxtaposed descriptions of "sweet" and "peculiar" was written in the *The Traveller*:

> Their chanting of the Lord's prayer and their rendering of "Home, Sweet, Home," were extremely sweet and musical .... But it was in the old-fashioned and peculiar hymns of the plantation slaves that the most striking development of their voices and powers was made. No one who has ever heard the negroes of the South in their religious songs can have any idea of the quaint, weird melody.
>
> (*The Traveller*, as cited in *American Missionary Supplement*, 1872, p. 3)

In Henry Ward Beecher's introduction of the Jubilee Singers in Boston, he stated, "Although they are respectable in rendering classical and other music ... they will give you an opportunity of hearing the peculiar slave songs, the spirituals and the praise songs" (*American Missionary Supplement*, 1872, p. 3). Similarly, while commenting on the musical training the singers received at their university, equating their "clear" voices with "culture" and "modification," the *Boston Journal* surmised that the singers still possessed that which was "different" for the White listener. "The singers have received sufficient culture to modify the complete abandon style of the old plantation, yet the natural, crystal clear melody of their voices retained sufficient of its original characteristics to charm the audience with its novelty" (*Boston Journal*, as cited in *American Missionary Supplement*, 1872, p. 3).

The "novelty" observed by the author of the *Boston Journal* article alludes to the "exotic" singing subject onto which the White listener imposes his conceptions of the singer. *The Newark Courier*'s description of the concert was that "the music and words were strange and weird .... They sang as if they couldn't help it" (*Newark Courier*, as cited in *American Missionary Supplement*, 1872, p. 1). From this account, the singing subject was depicted as one without control allowing the "disciplined" White listening subject to maintain superiority over the "irrational" and "undisciplined" Black bodies. A similar article in the *Brooklyn Daily Times*, with descriptions like "infection," and "wild pathetic strains," simultaneously derides and exoticizes the Black singing bodies.

> The singing was of a very high order .... Of these were the chorus from Ernani, "Hail us ye free" which was sung with a clearness and precision ... the feature of the evening, however, was the rendering of a number of camp meeting melodies ... we can testify that there is an infection in the devotion of these swarthy enthusiasts ... and the wild pathetic strains.
>
> (*Brooklyn Daily Times*, 1872, p. 2)

The need for the White listening subject to find "difference" in the Black singing subjects' performance of Western classical music aesthetics is evident in a *New York Times* review of a Fisk Jubilee concert ten years after their first concert tour. The choir was described as possessing "extraordinary skill and capacity in all that goes to make up good singing," however, the review goes on to say that "so much artificial refinement of tone, expression, and harmony has been added ... that some of the old charm has been sacrificed" (*New York Times*, 1882, p. 5). The success of the Fisk Jubilee singers to attain Western classical "artistic refinement" and "precision" ten years after their first concert tour, because of their Black bodies, however, was described as "artificial."

The complexity of the audience's reactions to the Fisk Jubilee choir's singing, much like the Carlisle Indian School's concerts, one might say, had little to do with the Fisk Jubilee Singers or the Carlisle Indian School

## 50 *Historical Overview*

students but rather the ways in which a White listening subject defines, perceives, and judges Black and Brown performers. For the Fisk Jubilee Singers to be accepted by White audiences, they had to sing and act according to Western classical rules; however, their performances, no matter how "precise" they became, were insufficient.

While audience reactions to concerts may seem trivial, they, in fact, shed light on the historical entanglement of racism, saviorism, assumed Western classical superiority, White superiority, and White fear of "Black advancement" (Love, 2019, p. 23). The historical conflation of class, moral superiority, and Western classical musical tastes allowed for a hierarchizing of people. This chapter has focused on the music teaching practices that have been used to advance ideological movements. The imposition of Western classical music teaching to "civilize" and "control" the receiver, under the guise of philanthropy and saviorism, was done so to reify hegemonic power structures. Whether the subject mastered the technique was inconsequential. Rather, an elite musical system afforded those privy to this musical system status and power and a separateness from the "unrefined." If the "civilizing" subject mastered the musical technique meant to "civilize" him, the teacher earned praise and recognition for his sacrificing endeavor. This is evident in the *American Missionary*'s description of the Fisk Jubilee performance:

> As the inspiring notes floated out upon the free air, we almost felt them to be choruses of thankfulness and triumph for the accomplishments and the promises in the great work of lifting up and educating an oppressed people. Let the faithful teachers in this University and kindred institutions take heart and hope in the great work which calls for so much personal sacrifice from them.
>
> *(American Missionary*, 1871, p. 113)

The "civilizing" subject, therefore, is always viewed in the civilizer's terms. The White listening subject, with the power to interpret the singer's performance, benefits from his status, thus making the recognition of the performer's ability a threat to his status. While the Fisk Jubilee singers acquiesced to the Western classical concert performance "standards" imposed upon them, their performance would never be adequately "standard" because of the bodies which they inhabited.

## References

Allen, R., Coker, D., & Champion, J. (1818). *The African Methodist Pocket Hymn Book*. Richard Allen for the African Methodist Connection.

*American Missionary* (1871, May). The Fisk University. *American Missionary*, 15(5), 113.

*American Missionary Supplement* (1872, March). Jubilee singers: Notices from the press. *American Missionary Supplement*, 16(3), 1–4.

*Baltimore Sun* (1894, April 10). Young Indians sightseeing. *Baltimore Sun*, 114(124), 2.

*Brooklyn Daily Times* (1872, January 4). The Jubilee Singers. *The Brooklyn Daily Times*, 2.

Catalogue of the Indian industrial school (1902). *Dickinson College Archives & Special Collections*. http://carlisleindian.dickinson.edu/publications/catalogue-indian-industrial-school-1902.

Civilization Fund Act (1819). 15th Cong. (1819).

Curwen, J. (1872). *The standard course of lessons and exercises in the Tonic Sol-fa method of teaching music*. Tonic Sol-Fa Agency.

Dunbar-Ortiz, R. (2014). *An indigenous peoples' history of the United States*. Beacon Press.

Embree, E. R. (1939). *Indians of the Americas*. Houghton Mifflin.

García, M. (1847). *Traité complet de l'art du chant en deux parties*. Heugel.

Grande, S. (2015). *Red pedagogy: Native American social and political thought*. Rowman & Littlefield.

Jones, C. C. (1842). *The religious instruction of the negroes in the United States*. Thomas Purse.

Love, B. L. (2019). *We want to do more than survive: Abolitionist teaching and the pursuit of educational freedom*. Beacon Press.

McBeth, S. (1983). *Ethnic identity and the boarding school experience*. University Press of America.

McBurney, S. (1891, February 1). *Musical Herald*, 515, 35–37.

Nabokov, P. (1999). *Native America testimony: A chronicle of Indian-White relations from prophesy to the present, 1492–2000*. Penguin Press.

*New York Times* (1882, January 17). The Jubilee Singers. *New York Times*, 31 (9473), 5.

Pratt, R. H. (1892). The advantages of mingling Indians with Whites. *Official Report of the Nineteenth Annual Conference of Charities and Correction*, 46–59. https://quod.lib.umich.edu/n/ncosw/ACH8650.1892.001?rgn=main;view=fulltext.

Seward, T. F. (1867). *The Temple choir: A collection of sacred and secular music, comprising a great variety of tunes, anthems, glees, elementary exercises and social songs, suitable for use in the choir, the singing school, and the social circle*. Mason Brothers.

Seward, T. F. (1872). *Jubilee songs: As sung by the Jubilee Singers of Fisk University*. Biglow & Main.

Seward, T. F. (1882a, June). Important announcement. *The Tonic Sol-fa Advocate*, 1 (10). 145–146.

Seward, T. F. (1882b, May). The Boston discussion. *The Tonic Sol-fa Advocate*, 1 (9), 129–134, 139.

Smith, M. (2001). Forever changed: Boarding school narratives of American Indian identity in the U.S. and Canada. *Indigenous Nations Studies Journal*, 2(2), 57–82.

Southern, E. (1977). Musical practices in Black churches of Philadelphia and New York, ca. 1800–1844. *Journal of the American Musicological Society*, 30(2), 296–312. doi:10.1525/jams.1977.30.2.03a00050.

*The Indian Helper* (1894, April 20). Return of the band and choir and observations on the way by one of the party. *The Indian Helper*, 9(30), 1–4.

*The Red Man* (1894, March–May). The band and choir make a little tour. *The Red Man*, 12(5), 3–6.

Volk, T. M. (2004). *Music, education, and multiculturalism: Foundations and principles*. Oxford University Press.

## 52 Historical Overview

Ward, A. (2000). *Dark midnight when I rise: The story of the Fisk Jubilee Singers*. Farrar, Straus, and Giroux.

Watson, J. L. (1819). *Methodist error, or, friendly, Christian advice: To those Methodists who indulge in extravagant religious emotions and bodily exercises*. D. & E. Fenton.

*Wilmington News* (1894, April 12). Educating the Indians. *Wilmington News*, 28(88), 4.

# 5 Character Improvement and Music Education in the United States

## Woodbridge and Fellenberg

Musical "civilizing" gave way to character "improvement" as music education became part of public school curricula in the United States. William Channing Woodbridge, one of the early pioneers of music education, advocated for vocal music to be incorporated into schools with the speech, "On Vocal Music as a Branch of Common Education," which he gave to the American Institute of Instruction (Jorgensen, 1984, p. 5). As editor of the journal *American Annals of Education and Instruction*, Woodbridge wrote extensively about the effects of music education on character improvement. He argued that music "has an effect which cannot be doubted, in softening and elevating the character" (Woodbridge, 1831, p. 67). In addition to character improvement, he believed that "the study of music, from its very nature cultivates the habits of order, and obedience, and union" (p. 67) and that "vocal music has no small influence on school discipline" (p. 67).

Woodbridge's equating of musical study with an "elevated" and "cultivated" character as well as discipline and obedience is much like Curwen's Tonic Sol-Fa mission to discipline and "civilize" the "uncivilized" through music teaching. To further articulate his belief that music should be part of public school instruction, Woodbridge used an anecdote from his travels to illustrate the influence of music on a person's character. "The editor has known and visited a village in Switzerland, where a set of drunken, disorderly young men were led, by the cultivation of vocal music among them, to an entire exterior reformation" (Woodbridge, 1831, p. 67). This experience, for Woodbridge, supported his belief that music instruction could "improve" and "elevate" a person's character. Deeply influenced by his travels to Switzerland and Germany, his encounters with educational leaders like Johann Heinrich Pestalozzi, Philipp Emanuel von Fellenberg, Michael Traugott Pfeiffer, and Hans Georg Nägeli, and his observations of Swiss and German schools (Jorgensen, 1984, p. 1), Woodbridge considered the European examples of music education as models of success. He wrote, "We were struck with the superior order and kindly aspect of the German schools in comparison with our own, and ascribed it not a little to the cultivation of music in them" (Woodbridge, 1831, p. 67).

DOI: 10.4324/9781003099475-7

## 54 Historical Overview

Woodbridge admired Fellenberg's philosophy of music education, which he interpreted as "character or moral development rather than musical development" (Jorgensen, 1984, p. 2). In his observations at Hofwyl, Fellenberg's school, Woodbridge idealized the ways in which music instruction "elevated" the characters of peasant children, "each of which was made to echo some truth, or point to some duty, by an appropriate song" (Woodbridge, 1833, p. 198). Truth and duty, Woodbridge believed, could therefore be attained through "appropriate" music instruction. Although Woodbridge's beliefs about music instruction, like Fellenberg's, were "utilitarian" in nature in which music provided a means by which to attain moral improvement, he did not ignore the importance of musical "taste" (Jorgensen, 1984, p. 3), as evidenced by his emphasis on "appropriate" musical instruction. Drawing from Fellenberg, Woodbridge believed that the cultivation of "proper" tastes in music, among other things would lead to moral betterment. According to Fellenberg, "A well-formed taste, a delicate esthetic judgement ... should be cultivated in the most careful and thorough manner" (Woodbridge, 1842, p. 300). The need for a student's tastes to be "well-formed" and "cultivated" implies a hierarchy of tastes thus necessitating a deliberate means by which to encourage taste improvement. For Fellenberg, music and design were vehicles with which to improve students' tastes; however, he cautioned that "the study of both should be carefully regulated" (Woodbridge, 1842, p. 300).

The hierarchizing of musical tastes and the regulation of musical study required the disciplining of students' music engagement. The "cultivated" musical taste to which students were to aspire was from the Western classical tradition. In his careful regulation of his students' musical tastes, not only did Fellenberg dictate which music was "appropriate" and how it should be studied, he also dictated the ways in which his students were permitted to experience music. The disciplining and regulation of musical tastes, therefore, allowed no room for the students' impressions. Rather, because Fellenberg believed that his students lacked "sound judgement," their character and moral improvement were dependent upon his instruction (Woodbridge, 1842, p. 122).

Following his European travels, Woodbridge returned to the United States convinced that American schools would greatly benefit from the replication of Fellenberg's and other European models of music education and "was intent on preserving the 'purity' and integrity" (Jorgensen, 1984, p. 4) of those models in the United States. Woodbridge's zeal for European music and teaching systems was well received. The climate to which he returned was saturated with reform and change within educational, musical, and religious spaces (p. 5). It was within this climate that Woodbridge gave his speech "On Vocal Music as a Branch of Common Education" "at the inaugural meeting of the American institute of Instruction" (p. 5). Lowell Mason's choir provided musical evidence for Woodbridge's argument.

## Mason and Pestalozzi

Mason, an avid music teacher, church musician, and composer, was profoundly impacted by Woodbridge's speech and adopted the pedagogies for which Woodbridge advocated. Their collaboration resulted in a book of songs for elementary music teaching called the *Juvenile Lyre*, which they published with their colleague, Elam Ives (Mark, 2008). The full title of the book, *Juvenile Lyre or Hymns and Songs, Religious, Moral and Cheerful, Set to Appropriate Music for the Use of Primary and Common Schools*, demonstrates their adoption of Fellenberg's and Pestalozzi's philosophies that music teaching with "appropriate" music would lead to moral "betterment." Referring to Woodbridge's observations of Fellenberg, the book's preface outlines the ways in which "appropriate" music and musical instruction can improve a person's character:

> It improves the heart. No one will question its power to soften the character and elevate the feelings ... by introducing vocal music among the youth ... it has been found materially to promote the Good order and discipline of the pupils; to render them more kind to each other, and more obedient to their teachers. The full influence of music is only felt where it is combined with appropriate words, and is employed in fixing useful instruction in the mind, and elevated and devotional feelings in the heart. Good or evil principles may be fixed most deeply by its influence.
>
> (Mason, 1835, pp. iv–v)

The publication of the *Juvenile Lyre* (1835), which summarized Mason's and Woodbridge's philosophy of music education, was consequential in their advocacy for music education in schools. With this philosophical rationale, Mason sought a means by which to infuse "dignity and strength to the movement" (Seward, 1889, p. 14). With the help of "a number of leading citizens" (p. 14), Mason founded the Boston Academy of Music. As a member of the Boston Academy of Music, Mason then published the *Manual of the Boston Academy of Music: For Instruction in the Elements of Vocal Music, on the System of Pestalozzi* (1836). According to Mason, the purpose of the book was to, "diminish the obstacles which impeded the progress of those who wish to acquire a correct knowledge of the art" (Mason, 1836, p. iii). The manual, therefore, would provide the reader, "all the knowledge requisite for the correct performance of vocal music" (p. iii). From the outset, Mason articulates his belief that there is only one "correct" way of singing, for which his manual would provide the technique. With this manual, Mason called on music teachers to be vigilant in assessing "good" and "bad" singing. "Proper" and "correct" singing is described as a "pure" and a "good tone" (p. 97), which can be recognized by a person with a "musical ear," all of which are "the result of cultivation" (p. 16). Mason advised music teachers to correct

## 56  Historical Overview

"bad" singing by themselves mimicking their students' voices and modeling the "bad" and the "good" sound (p. 100).

In addition, as teachers assessed and corrected their students' singing, Mason (1836) suggested that the teacher rank the students based upon their singing and musical "cultivation" into four "classes." The first two "classes" denoted singers who had accomplished or were close to accomplishing the "correct" way of singing and who possessed a "good" musical ear. Mason stipulated that the third class of singers described students "whose ear is somewhat defective, and whose voices are comparatively uncertain [but with] proper instruction, and perseverance these may become correct singers" (p. 101). The fourth "class" described "those who, wither on account of defective organs, or the entire destitution of a musical ear, cannot without great difficulty be made to sing" (p. 101) and "cannot be advised to attempt the cultivation of music" (p. 102). It seems appropriate that within the vocal hierarchy of "good" and "bad" singing, students were separated into "classes," where the first class was most familiar with the Western classical vocal technique. Whether or not Mason intentionally used the term "class" to indicate a "caste" of singers is irrelevant. What is relevant is that the ranking and judging of students' voices and bodies became synonymous with the teaching of "proper" vocal technique in the music classroom.

Much like Curwen's, Mason's (1836) instructions are militaristic in tone, equating a contrived posture and mouth opening with a "correct," "natural" singing technique. Students were "to stand erect, with the head looking directly forward, the breast bending a little outwards, and the mouth duly open … so far that the end of the fore finger may have free play between the teeth" (p. 100). For Mason, the risk of not enforcing "proper" vocal technique was "faulty" (p. 100) singing, which would lead to an "unacceptable" performance. The final musical "product," therefore, was the priority. This priority is articulated by Seward (1889) in his description of the rationales behind Mason's life's work, which were the "improvement of church music" and "teaching children to sing intelligently" (p. 10). Both goals to which he aspired prioritized the product over the process, and in doing so, the singer. The singer was a function of the product but without agency or the ability to choose vocal options outside of the realm of the Western classical technique. Much like Curwen, Mason devised teaching manuals to improve the musical product, whether it be singing in church or a choral performance. Improvement was incumbent upon the vocal subject(s) adhering to the discipline of vocal teaching.

Mason drew on Pestalozzi's educational philosophy with his emphasis on the effect of music on a person's character and feelings, stating that "the chief object of the cultivation of vocal music is to train the feelings" (Mason, 1836, p. 24). Pestalozzi likened music to "one of the most effective aids of moral education" (Pestalozzi, 1827, as cited in Keene, 1982, p. 85) because of the "most beneficial influence of music on the feelings" where, according to Pestalozzi, "if cultivated in the right spirit, it strikes at the root of every bad or narrow feeling, or every ungenerous or mean propensity, or every emotion unworthy of humanity" (p. 86). Pestalozzi, although not a music educator himself, sought help from Pfeiffer and Nägeli to devise a singing manual based on his educational theory (p. 83). An advocate for child-centered learning, Pestalozzi suggested that educators encourage children to "express [themselves] on the subject" (p. 83). Had he known how to write a music manual, Pestalozzi might have encouraged children to express their musical identities irrespective of the sound. His concern was with the child and not the musical product. Pfeiffer and Nägeli's manual entitled *Method of Teaching Singing According to Pestalozzian Principles* (p. 84), however, deduced Pestalozzi's theory to a teacher-centered, discipline-focused, regimented vocal pedagogy.

Keene (1982) notes that "suddenly from the generalities of Pestalozzi's philosophy came a set of mandated rules for the instruction of music" (Keene, 1982, p. 84). The manual stipulated that teachers use terminology like "correct" and "incorrect" as well as "clear" and "unclear" to describe the musical sound. "Each step was prescribed, and nowhere was there any mention of ideas the children might have had concerning the music they were to study. All direction came from the teacher ... and the children followed" (p. 84). In his discussion of Pfeiffer and Nägeli's manual, Pestalozzi distinguished between musical "proficiency" and musical feeling (Pestalozzi, 1827, as cited in Keene, 1982, p. 85). Pestalozzi exclaimed, "it is not this proficiency which I would describe as a desirable accomplishment of education" but rather the "influence of music on the feelings" (p. 85). Pfeiffer and Nägeli's manual, with a hierarchical approach to music teaching in which proficiency and musical product were prioritized over the child, therefore, was an inaccurate application of Pestalozzi's philosophy to music education.

Mason's own manual, *For Instruction in the Elements of Vocal Music, on the System of Pestalozzi* (1836), draws heavily on Pfeiffer and Nägeli's manual. For Mason and Nägeli, the musical aims for a singing manual were to encourage musical proficiency and improve musical performance. This emphasis required that the teacher's role be authoritative and the student subservient, leaving no room for the student's musical identity and therefore in opposition to Pestalozzi's philosophy. Pestalozzi's belief that music could improve children's moral character, however, did fit nicely into Mason's mission for vocal and moral improvement through music; although, Mason clearly defined *which* music and singing style would lead to moral improvement. "We should see that the songs of your families are pure in sentiment and truthful in musical taste. Avoid Negro melodies and comic songs for most of their tendencies is to corrupt both musically and morally" (Mason, 1822, as cited in Colwell, 1985, p. 22).

## Mason's Influence and the Moral Imperative

From the moment of their inception into the public school system, Mason's music education methods and the underlying ideology from which the

## 58  Historical Overview

methods were formed were based on musical and moral superiority. The "appropriate" musical technique would ensure moral improvement. It was because of this ideology, that music was considered for public schools. In response to petitions submitted "to the Boston School Committee, asking that vocal music be introduced into the school curriculum" (Mark, 2008, p. 45), one of which was from Mason and the Boston Academy of Music, in 1837, the committee accepted the petitions on an experimental basis. They justified their decision based upon what they deemed to be a moral imperative—the impact of music on a person's morality—deeming music instruction necessary as a means of "governing" students' morality (p. 46). The experimental trial to which the committee agreed consisted of Mason teaching music for one year at the Hawes School, after which a report would be formulated (Mark, 2008). At the end of the academic year, the report in fact determined that Mason's music teaching made a positive impact. Among the descriptions of success, the report noted the "great moral effect of vocal music" (p. 47). The success of Mason's teaching led to the Boston School Committee's approval of music "as a subject of the public school curriculum" (p. 48). Mason was given the role of Super-intendent of Music and to this day is considered by many as "the father of singing among the children" (p. 34) and "the most important figure in American music education" (Keene, 1982, p. 102).

The influence of Mason's music teaching manuals and resources as well as his music teaching philosophy on music education today is far greater than one might expect. The pedagogy with which he taught singing, his belief system about "appropriate" music, "proper" singing, and the influence of "good" music on morality are all embedded in the assumptions, ideology, and belief system with which modern day music education is immersed. Mason's role in embedding the *bel canto* vocal technique into music teaching practice and normalizing Garcia's operatic aesthetics within K-12 music education, however, is perhaps the most salient. The impact of the *bel canto* vocal technique on modern day music education practices cannot be overstated. It was the indiscriminate adoption and application of *bel canto* vocal principles, by Mason, Curwen, and their contemporaries, to primary music teaching that have had a lasting impact on music education, leading to the disciplining, silencing, and racializing of students' voices in the music classroom.

## References

Colwell, R. J. (1985). Program evaluation in music teacher education. *The Bulletin of the Council for Research in Music Education*, 81, 18–62.

Jorgensen, E. R. (1984). William Channing Woodbridge's lecture, "On vocal music as a branch of common education" revisited. *Studies in Music*, 18, 1–32.

Keene, J. A. (1982). *A history of music education in the United States*. University Press of New England.

Mark, M. L. (2008). *A concise history of American music education*. Rowman & Littlefield.

## Character Improvement and Music Education  59

Mason, L. (1835). *Juvenile lyre: Or hymns and songs, religious, moral, and cheerful, set to appropriate music.* Carter, Hendee, & Co.

Mason, L. (1836). *Manual of the Boston Academy of Music: For instruction in the elements of vocal music, on the system of Pestalozzi.* J. H. Wilkins & R. B. Carter.

Seward, T. F. (1889). *The educational work of Dr. Lowell Mason.* A. W. Thayer.

Woodbridge, W. (1831). Music, as a branch of common education. *American Annals of Education,* 1(2), 64–67.

Woodbridge, W. (1833). On vocal music as a branch of common education. *American Annals of Education,* 3(5), 193–213.

Woodbridge, W. (1842). *Letters from Hofwyl.* Longman, Brown, Green, and Longmans.

# 6 Music Education Standardization and Codification

## Methods

John Curwen and Lowell Mason, with their music and vocal teaching manuals, catalyzed the movement to standardize, codify, and disseminate music teaching methods. By the end of the nineteenth century, influential music teachers were vouching for room within the saturated publishing market (Mark, 2008). With their opposing views on "rote" versus "note" methods, Luther Whiting Mason, Frederick Ripley, Thomas Tapper, John Tufts, and Hosea Holt had successfully published three competing methods: The *National Music Course* (Mason, 1894); the *Natural Music Course* (Ripley & Tapper, 1895); and the *Normal Music Course* (Tufts & Holt, 1888). Despite their theoretical contestations, within these differing theoretical approaches, the voice teaching is remarkably the same. The vocal pedagogy to which each music teaching method subscribed was adopted from Garcia, through John Curwen and Lowell Mason.

### Music Courses and Vocal Pedagogy

L.W. Mason (1894) emphasized the importance of a "good quality of voice" with a "clear," "sweet" tone quality and the need to "cultivate" the ear so as to avoid "faulty" vocal sounds (pp. 7–10). Much like his predecessors, including his teacher, Lowell Mason, he believed that music teaching should "cultivate the ear, the voice, and the musical taste" (p. 10) of the student. He also considered a disciplined, staid body to be important for producing good singing. For L.W. Mason, singing should "not be cumbered with meaningless and otherwise useless muscular jerking or pantomime" (p. 16), perhaps referring to dancing. Further, even the most "acceptable" form of movement, marching, should not be combined with singing. L.W. Mason clearly draws from Lowell Mason's adoption of Garcia's *bel canto* vocal technique. In addition, he also emphasizes the influence music has on morals and tastes, drawing from Lowell Mason's adaptation of Pestalozzian philosophy.

Ripley and Tapper (1895), in the Natural Music Course, although differing from L.W. Mason theoretically, perpetuate the same vocal teaching

DOI: 10.4324/9781003099475-8

methods as L.W. Mason and their predecessors. They emphasized the importance of a "soft" "proper quality of tone" which should be "free from harsh nasal sounds" (p. 4) and should be produced with an "erect" (p. 4) posture. In their discussion about "proper" vocal technique, they quote Mathilde Marchesi, one of Garcia's students. "There are but two of them in the world, the good and the bad; exactly so there exist only two singing methods, the efficient and the deficient" (p. 4). In applying the *bel canto* school of thought to their music education manual, they reduce children's singing to "good" and "bad," "efficient" and "deficient," based upon the aesthetics of the *bel canto* technique.

Although they advocated for a different theoretical approach, Tufts and Holt (1888), in the third competing music education text, applied the same vocal principles. They emphasized "a proper use of the voice" (p. 15) to avoid "harsh and noisy singing, so ruinous to ear and voice" (p. 17). According to Tufts and Holt, teachers were to teach "correct habits in using the voice, good phrasing, distinct articulation, and accurate pronunciation" (p. 13) and "a good position of the body" (p. 17). Much like the authors of the competing texts, they also cautioned against movement with singing. "Children should never be required to sing while marching, or when calisthenic or gymnastic exercises are made" (p. 13). If teachers adhered to these rules and their "suggestions about the proper management of children's voices" (p. 17) then, according to Tufts and Holt, they would reap the benefits of music "morally, mentally, and physically" (p. 11).

## Musical Saviorism and Universalism

The belief that Western classical music education could "save" or "improve" a student's character continued throughout the twentieth century. Musical saviorism, although taking on a different character from that of the previous centuries, was a driving force for music education. One of the musical "prophets," or "missionaries" as he was so affectionately described (*The New Republic* and *The Outlook*, as cited in Perryman, 1972, p. 236), Walter Damrosch was described in the *New York Times* in 1950 as the "Evangel of Music" (Downes, 1950, p. X7). With his music education radio show, Damrosch championed Western classical music education and reached music classrooms throughout the United States and Canada (Howe, 2003). Much like other "evangelical" musical movements, like the Tonic Sol-Fa and ABRSM systems, Damrosch's influence was extensive. The music teaching materials that supplemented his radio show—the student notebooks and teacher's manuals—were distributed throughout the United States, "South Africa, Japan, China, the Dutch West Indies, the Philippines, Chile, France, Iraq, Canada, and Mexico" (Royal & LaPrade, 1933, as cited in Howe, 2003, p. 73). Within one school year, from 1933 to 1934, "103,175 student notebooks ... and 13,700 instructor's manuals were sold" (p. 73).

62    *Historical Overview*

Damrosch's influence on the field of music education in the United States cannot be understated, as "he was given a nationwide stage to teach America's schoolchildren about music" (Gregory, 2016, p. 302). The ideology on which his broadcasts and music teaching materials were based perpetuated the "superiority" of Western classical music education. Like the Social Darwinists of his time, Damrosch proclaimed that "art develops not by revolution but by evolution" (press release prepared by Damrosch in the Damrosch Collection (NYRL), as cited in Perryman, 1972, p. 225), thus claiming that Western classical music was the most evolved. It was this assumption that undergirded his claim that music—Western classical music, that is—was a universal language and should be taught universally. With this philosophy, he endeavored to, in his own words, "spread its gospel" (*New York Times*, 1946, p. 1). In addition to his broadcasts being filled with sentiments of musical universality (Martin, 1983), Damrosch, with Hugh Gartlan and Karl Gehrkens, published the *Universal Music Series*, a series of music education method books (Mark, 2008, p. 69). Much like other method books of the time, the *Universal Music Series* stipulated explicit instructions for the teacher to ensure that the method was enacted "correctly." They advised that "to make success certain it will be necessary that you, the teacher, read, digest, and put into practice all the directions and suggestions given in this book" (Damrosch et al., 1923, p. vii).

Damrosch et al. (1923) claimed the universality of their method. That is, if the teacher followed the rules, then the method could unquestionably be applied to any context with any demographic of students. Teachers were not only instructed to carefully follow the lesson plans, but they were also given explicit directions about how to behave in the music classroom. "Always use good music for the listening lesson, have it as well rendered as possible, and see to it that both teacher and children listen quietly, attentively, and thoughtfully" (p. vii). The focus on a quiet listening body is reminiscent of music education method books of the nineteenth century where the student's body was disciplined and controlled in the music classroom. The twentieth-century methods books, however, sought to discipline both the students' *and* teachers' bodies. These method books written by leaders in the music education field, like Damrosch, created a hegemonic system of power within the field of music education, where methods and standards took precedence over teachers' creativity and agency. The specificity of what was deemed "correct" in music teaching and performing, therefore, provided a means by which to control students and teachers alike. In the *Universal Music Series* (1923) teachers were instructed to "speak often to the children concerning the *beauty* of the songs that they are singing, and try to inculcate the ideal of singing them *beautifully* as well as *correctly*" (Damrosch et al., 1923, p. 4).

Damrosch's conception of "correct" singing is emphasized throughout the teacher's manual and described as "soft and sweet" (Damrosch et al., 1923, p. 5). Drawing from Garcia and his predecessors, he describes the "voice quality" and "beauty of tone" (p. 5) that teachers should encourage with "correct bodily posture" (p. 5). In addition to requiring "correct" singing and posture, the manual required that teachers choose repertoire that was deemed acceptable by Damrosch. When "selecting records," teachers were told "never buy what is commonly known as 'popular' music or any kind of unworthy selections, and do not allow the children to bring such records from home" (p. 35). Additionally, teachers were to "pronounce the titles and names before the composition is given, being sure the pronunciation is correct" (p. 35). Damrosch believed that music education could improve a person's character, and that music has the "power to 'tone up' both mind and body" (Damrosch et al., 1923, p. 1). The means to the end, the method and specific musical paradigm with which character improvement could take place, however, took precedence over the student and teacher.

### Adolescent Voice Teaching

Other popular manuals of the time focused on the particularities of adolescent vocal teaching. William Tomlins, an esteemed children's choir director and voice teacher, published the Laurel Series of songs (1900) in which he advocated for his vocal teaching method. So popular was his approach that "his work became the standard for teaching children to sing" (Mark, 2008, p. 68).

In the introduction to his 1919 *Laurel Music-Reader* publication, Tomlins described his vocal teaching method. One of his pedagogical beliefs about which he felt strongly and which he reiterated throughout the introduction concerned the "natural and properly produced voice" (Tomlins, 1919, p. iv). Tomlins believed that the *head voice* was the only "natural and properly produced voice" (p. iv). He strongly articulated that

> *any other voice is false, forced, disagreeable, and injurious ... therefore when the head voice is used for every tone high and low throughout the entire range, producing one unbroken register, then, and only then, is the voice properly produced.*
>
> (p. iv, original emphasis)

Tomlins' zealous belief that children should only be instructed to sing using their head voice became common practice throughout the twentieth century and continues to inform music teachers today. The positioning of a vocal aesthetic, the head voice, as more "proper" and "appropriate" for children's singing allows for a hierarchy of vocal aesthetics. The head voice singing aesthetic for which Tomlins, a British choral conductor, and others throughout the century advocated is a marking of Western classical choral culture. For many singing traditions outside of this musical paradigm, the head voice aesthetic is unfamiliar and rarely used. Therefore, the emphasis on an exclusively head voice production for school music teaching allows for a ranking of vocal aesthetics and traditions, thus communicating the believed superiority of Western classical singing aesthetics.

## 64  *Historical Overview*

With the demarcation of a "correct" and "incorrect" vocal production came the partitioning of singers into categories of "singers" and "non-singers." The ranking of children's voices was based upon the children's ability to conform to Western classical aesthetics of vocal production. In her popular series for elementary music teaching, entitled *The World of Music* (1936), Mabelle Glenn (Mark, 2008, p. 70) describes the singer classification system with which she delineates three categories of singers: "a. Those who can sing a melody. b. Those who can follow the melody but do not sing accurately (near singers). c. Those who seem to be unable to sing even a single tone correctly (non-singers)" (Glenn, 1936, p. 6). The description of a "non-singer" was, therefore, a singer who could not sing a tone "correctly." The ways in which Glenn and her contemporaries defined a "correct" tone were based on vocal aesthetics rooted in the Western classical singing tradition. Children, therefore, came to believe that their singing voice was inadequate because of these narrow criteria of "correctness."

### *"Good" Musical Taste and Music Appreciation*

In addition to "provid[ing] opportunity for training in the correct use of the voice"—where correct is narrowly defined by Western classical vocal aesthetics—the purpose of *The World of Music* series was to "cultivate good musical taste … and promote song appreciation and interpretation" (Glenn, 1936, p. 2). Like Damrosch and other music educators of the early nineteenth century, Glenn was concerned with imparting "good" musical taste to elementary music students. The nineteenth-century conflation of musical tastes and morality gave way to the twentieth-century discourses of *music appreciation* and character, where music appreciation signified the ability to recognize that which was deemed musically "superior." Music appreciation, therefore, was synonymous with musical "taste" from a Western classical musical perspective. Those who appreciated "good" music exhibited "good" musical taste and therefore "good" character. Glenn (1936) describes music appreciation as "an appreciation of good music through listening to only the best music" (p. 4), the "best" music being Western classical music.

The "widely adopted" (Mark, 2008, p. 69) *Progressive Music Series*, by Horatio Parker, Osbourne McConathy, Edward Birge, and Otto Miessner was based on a similar ideology. The authors outline the underlying belief system on which they based their educational methods, asserting that "the molding of character, the development of high ideals, and the forming of good taste and artistic discrimination are of great importance" (Parker et al., 1918, p. 4). Parker et al.'s description of that which would lead to character improvement was rooted in elitism and "high society." "Good" musical tastes, "high" ideals and the ability to discriminate between that which is musically "good" and "bad" were requisite for character development and therefore should be prioritized in music teaching. In addition, they emphasized the importance of cultivating in students "a discriminating taste for the best in music" which "will enable the student[s] to discriminate between that which is worthy and that which is unworthy" (p. 15).

Parker, Damrosch, and the music education leaders of the time codified and standardized music teaching method books, musical appreciation, discrimination, and taste based upon the assumption that Western classical music methods were superior. This assumption was considered an objective truth and justified with the scientific and evolutionary beliefs of the time.

## Bureaucratization

The twentieth-century ideological entanglement of standards, tastes, and character improvement, born out of the "civilizing," "saving," and morality of the nineteenth century, perpetuated the believed superiority of a Western classical music epistemology, albeit in new forms and utterances. The civilizing mission became standardization, codification, uniformity, universality, and music appreciation. The fervor for music methods, standards, conformity, and universality coincided with assimilationism in the United States in the first part of the twentieth century. With increased immigration, education was used to inculcate immigrants with American ideology, mannerisms, and culture and, as Mark notes, "music was an important part of the process" (Mark, 2008, p. 97).

### Music Supervisors National Conference and Standards

It was within this political and educational climate that the founding of the first official organization for music educators in the United States took place. Music education leaders like Gherkins, who collaborated with Damrosch to produce the *Universal Music Series* (1923), as well as Birge and McConathy of the *Progressive Music Series* (1914), were at the forefront of the establishment. With their methods and ideology, and within an educational climate of cultural assimilation, in 1910, the National Association for Music Education (NAfME)—which was first called the Music Supervisors National Conference (MSNC)—was founded.

The organization "came into existence as an eventual result of a conference of public school music supervisors" in 1907 (Molnar, 1955, p. 40). The purpose for the initial meeting of school music supervisors was to "inspect and discuss a new" (p. 40) music teaching method. By 1914, the first *Music Supervisors' Bulletin* was published to chronicle the discussions which took place at, and in response to, the annual meetings. The goals outlined in the first issue demonstrated the belief system on which MSNC was founded. Giddings, the host of the 1914 conference, summarized the urgency of the goals outlined by MSNC. "The tremendously important work of building up a musical people is in the hands of the music supervisors" ("By our host," 1914, p. 6). This "important work," according to Giddings, required "efficiency" and standardization. He stated, "as a first

## 66   Historical Overview

step toward efficiency we should standardize our methods. The National Supervisor's Conference should be able to say authoritatively that they have agreed upon the best way to teach music in the schools" (p. 6). The MSNC's authority would then allow them, according to Giddings, to "say to the educators of the country 'This is the way it should be done and these are the results to be attained' ... 'This is the best way to teach music in the schools'" (p. 6).

Giddings encapsulated the urgency felt by the MSNC organization to improve music teaching in the United States. Their saviorist and authoritative mission to "build up a musical people" was one of standardization and efficiency in which music education was reduced to "This is the way it should be done and these are the results to be attained" (*Music Supervisors' Bulletin*, 1914, p. 6). The delineation of universal standards and a standardized method ensured that the governing body, those who developed the standards and the methods, would maintain control over the music teachers to whom these standards were disseminated. The MSNC organization was founded on a hierarchical power structure, where assimilation, uniformity, universality, and standards were deemed a necessary means by which to improve music teaching and learning and to, as stated by Giddings, "present a united front to the world" (p. 6).

In 1921, the MSNC Educational Council presented the standards they determined to be "a desirable ideal for all schools" (Journal of Proceedings, 1921, p. 216). These standards set the precedent for decades to come. The MSNC's standards explicitly defined the aims, materials, procedures, and attainments for each grade level. Although some of the language had changed to reflect contemporary educational discourse, the aims, ideals, and beliefs on which the music standards were based were largely representative of the music teaching ideology of Lowell Mason, Curwen, and the influencers of the nineteenth century. Western classical music, pedagogy, and beliefs about listening and singing were prioritized. For the first three years of instruction, an emphasis was put on "correct" listening and singing as well as the development of a "good" musical taste. "Correct" listening was conceived as listening with a still and quiet body and voice. The aim was to "to cultivate the power of careful, sensitive aural attention" (Journal of Proceedings, 1921, p. 222). This required the disciplining of students' bodies and voices and the discouragement of musical body entrainment. The standards specified that listening activities should only include "good musical compositions" (p. 225). "Good" music consisted of Western classical music compositions with which teachers were to cultivate in their students an "appreciation of music" (p. 222). An "appreciation for music" to which the standards referred was a specific propensity and taste for Western classical musical aesthetics. This was described as "developing an intelligent musical taste and judgment" (p. 230).

The goal, outlined in the standards, was for students "to prefer compositions that have real musical merit and charm to those that are weak or common" and "to listen to good compositions for the sheer joy and charm of their beauty" (Journal of *Proceedings*, 1921, p. 224). The teaching of music appreciation, therefore, was the inculcation of the superiority of Western classical music. The preference for Western classical music aesthetics was also emphasized in the teaching of singing. The standards instructed teachers to "direct[ing] aural attention to beauty of tone in singing" to encourage the "preference on the part of the children for good tones rather than bad" (p. 223). Thus, the cultivation of a "music appreciation" also required that students develop a preference for the vocal aesthetics of the *bel canto* singing tradition. This vocal technique was emphasized throughout the standards whereby teachers were directed to monitor, assess, control, and even "cure" children's vocal habits (p. 223) with "frequent examination[s] of all voices individually" (p. 230) "as a means of confirming and establishing individual capability" (p. 229).

Teachers were given authority to rank and assess the talent and capability of each student based upon their perceptions and understanding of Western classical vocal aesthetics. The subjectivity of vocal beauty was standardized and codified. Teachers were to aim for their students to "sing correctly and pleasingly" (Journal of *Proceedings*, 1921, p. 224), "using light head tones" (p. 222) and "without harmful" and "bad vocal habits" (p. 224). The MSNC vocal teaching, inherited from Lowell Mason and Curwen required that the teacher "correct" and "free" children's voices from "harmful vocal habits." Vocal teaching, therefore, was based on a presupposition that children's voices, in their natural state, were in need of fixing. Vocal teaching in schools would "correct" children's vocal expressions of their cultural and musical backgrounds. Assimilation and Americanization, when applied to music teaching, meant replacing ones vocal identity with "correct" singing. Teachers were to "correct" their students' singing with "close attention" and "careful treatment" so as to prevent further harmful singing.

Discourses of vocal "care" and "harm" in 1921 were precursors of today's discourses of vocal "health." Both in 1921 and the present, it seems absurd that one might contest the importance of "health" and "care" in vocal teaching; however, it is the seemingly obvious, incontestable normalization of "healthy" singing that has allowed for a vocal hegemony within elementary music teaching and the justified "correction" of children's vocal identities. The ideology that Western classical singing is assumed to be healthiest perpetuates a vocal hierarchy and the supposed superiority of the *bel canto* singing technique. The prioritization of this ideology within music education leads to the homogenization of children's voices and destruction of their vocal-cultural identities. It is, once again, however, the saviorist ideology of vocal betterment and vocal health that indoctrinates practitioners, even those with the best intentions, into believing that vocal homogenization and "correction" is in the best interest of all students.

Vocal hegemony in music education, championed by Lowell Mason, reaffirmed by the MSNC, and rampant in music teaching today is contemporary assimilationism, perpetuated because of saviorist, misinterpreted

68   *Historical Overview*

notions of vocal health. Historical context and the tracing of assumptions throughout history allow us to take a critical view of that which we have come to believe is true.

The MSNC's first codification of music education standards provided the foundation upon which all subsequent revisions were based, thus influencing music education practice in the United States for decades to come. Within the same landmark document in which the MSNC standards were unveiled, the MSNC also outlined admission criteria for music teacher education programs. Students were expected to have had high school music courses and the ability to perform on the piano "at least the difficulty of two grades" (Journal of Proceedings, 1921, p. 219). They were expected to be able to sight sing "material at least of the difficulty of ordinary hymn and folk tunes" as well as "take down tonal dictation of moderate difficulty" (p. 219). In addition, it was stipulated that "only persons [who] have an agreeable singing voice and a fairly quick sense of tone and rhythm [would] be admitted" (p. 219). The criteria, based on a Western classical epistemology, were culturally specific. The acceptable candidate for music teacher education programs would have studied piano, presumably privately, taken music courses in high school, be able to sight-sing, and dictate, upon hearing, music that was played. In addition, the qualified candidate would sing with a Western classical vocal aesthetic. The MSNC admission criteria, therefore, set the stage for auditions and gatekeeping well into the twenty-first century, justifying the admission or rejection of candidates based upon their social, musical and financial capital. Because admission to music teacher education programs is "the only available pipeline to K-12 music teaching" (Koza, 2008, p. 152), the admission criteria that require candidates to have the means with which to access private lessons, a high school with music courses, and the cultural background of which Western classical music is a part, contribute to the whiteness of the field.

The affinity of the 1921 criteria with admission criteria in the twenty-first century cannot be ignored, as issues of access and equity are salient topics within music teacher education programs in the United States. Not only did the MSNC describe the type of person that should be accepted into music teacher education programs, they also described the type of work the music educator would undertake upon graduation. Included within this list was the obligation to "take charge of community singing with all its possibilities in the direction of inspiration, socialization and Americanization" (Journal of Proceedings, 1921, p. 220). Therefore, according to the MSNC, the influence of a successful music educator would reach well beyond the realm of the school building into the community. Parents and children alike, through singing, would be encouraged to abandon the musical tongues of their ancestors for the Americanized, homogenized Western classical choral aesthetic. Music education and assimilationism shared a common goal—to whitewash America. By the end of the twentieth century, the "melting pot" rhetoric of the first part of the century would give way to multiculturalism

*Standardization and Codification* 69

and inclusivity (Volk, 2004, p. 113). The assimilationist, homogenous, ideological underpinnings of music education, however, would live on in contemporary music education discourses, albeit in less overt terms.

## Methods and Philosophy

In 1934, the Music Supervisors National Conference became the Music Educators National Conference (MENC) (Mark, 2008, p. 101), a name that would remain until 2011, when MENC would adopt its current title, The National Association for Music Education (NAfME) (NAfME, n.d.). MENC's influence on music teaching practice and standardization grew exponentially throughout the second half of the twentieth century and into the twenty-first century. In 1947, MENC began to publish *Music Education Source Books*, which in book form disseminated "the materials developed by MENC commissions since 1942" (Mark, 2008, p. 108). The source books, like MENC's other publications, greatly impacted music education in the United States. In addition, MENC's influence on the methods and "standards" being implemented in music teaching throughout the United States was expansive. The widespread use of the Orff and Kodály methods was largely due to their visibility at MENC conferences and their subsequent alliance with MENC (Mark, 2020, p. 9). The fervor for music methods, source books, standards, and curriculum was endemic of this period, although many of the methods perpetuated the same ideology of the previous 100 years. In the Introduction of the English adaptation of the first volume of Orff's Schulwerk, *Music for Children* ([1950]1956), Walter, the translator, describes the philosophy behind Orff's music teaching approach:

> That the growth of music must be re-enacted in a growing human being; that a child must be led through the various stages (from the most primitive to the more complex) which man traversed before music reached the level on which we find it now.
>
> (Orff & Keetman, [1950]1956, Introduction section, para. 2)

Walter's interpretation of the philosophical underpinnings of the Orff Schulwerk method demonstrates the ways in which Social Darwinism and discourses about musical evolution penetrated educational thought and practice. "'Primitive' music was considered to be the lower end of the musical evolution, folk music slightly higher, and fine art music at the top of the evolutionary ladder" (Volk, 2004, p. 29).

Orff's method incorporated rhythm, repetition, percussion instruments, and the pentatonic scale. His method was based upon, in his words, "elemental" and "primitive" music-making techniques. In the Preface to *Music for Children* ([1950]1956), Orff provides the rationale for the melodic material he used. "The melodies are pentatonic throughout. Music based on a five tone scale represents a stage of development which closely corresponds to the

70 *Historical Overview*

mentality of children" (Orff & Keetman, [1950]1956, Preface section, para. 2). The pentatonic scale, used in diverse music traditions throughout the world, in Orff's estimation, is evolutionarily inferior and therefore appropriate for beginning music instruction. The frequent use of *ostinati*—repeated rhythmic or musical patterns—in the Orff method is practiced because, according to Orff, "the use of ostinati leads quite naturally to simple forms of polyphony" (Orff & Keetman, [1950]1956, Preface section, para. 5). Ostinati, a foundational rhythmic element of many African music traditions, among others, therefore, according to Orff, is merely a stage in musical development towards more complicated polyphony, found within Western classical music. The mallet percussion instruments and drums used in the Orff method—instruments widely used in musical traditions world-wide—are reduced to pedagogical elements. According to Orff, "Even the simplest instruments require a certain amount of technique and practicing" (Orff & Keetman, [1950]1956, Preface section, p. 2, para. 6).

Orff's music teaching method, therefore, is based on the infantilization and reduction of music-making practices common to diverse musical traditions throughout the world. While the music-making techniques may lend themselves well to teaching, it is the erasure of the cultural source and deeming of the musical practice as "primitive," "elemental," and "simple" that makes the philosophy on which Orff's method is based problematic. This philosophy is evident in Orff's description of the purpose of his method. "It is the over-all aim of this book, to teach, as in a primer, a vocabulary so basic, that it underlies all genuine understanding of the language of music" (Orff & Keetman, [1950]1956, Preface section, p. 2, para. 7). This method, according to Walter, "cannot be achieved by ... sophisticated material of the classical variety" (Orff & Keetman, [1950]1956, Introduction section, p. 2, para. 5). The Orff method, based on a hierarchizing of music-making practices and the superiority of Western classical music practices, reflects the philosophical undertones of the time in which it was created. Social Darwinism, Eugenics, and the ranking of peoples and cultures were all part and parcel of this time. The question to consider, therefore, is whether the Orff music teaching method, with its underlying philosophy, is beneficial for today's music teachers and students.

Much like the Orff method, the Kodály method of music education is widely used worldwide without much attention to the underlying philosophical assumptions on which the method was based. In his writings on music education, Kodály lamented the state of musical "taste" in Hungarian society, equating society's musical ignorance to a love for "trashy literature in music" and an inclination to "flee" from "refined" music (Kodály, [1964]1974, p. 119). Kodály chastised Hungarian society, who "can very well distinguish between inferior and vintage wines" for choosing "inferior wine in music" (Kodály, [1964]1974, p. 119). He, therefore, considered a "refined" musical taste to be indispensable for Hungarian society because in his words:

Bad taste in art is a veritable sickness of the soul. It seals the soul off from contact with masterpieces and from the life-giving nourishment emanating from them without which the soul wastes away or become stunted, and the whole character of the man is branded with a peculiar mark.

(Kodály, [1964]1974, p. 120)

Music of the masters—Western classical music—according to Kodály, would improve the characters and souls of his fellow Hungarians.

In his discussion about the musical state of Hungary, he poses the question, "What is to be done?", to which he suggests music education in schools as a means to "instill a thirst for finer music" in children (Kodály, [1964] 1974, p. 120). The purpose of the Kodály method was to instill in children a predisposition for Western classical music as a means to "improve" their musical taste. Kodály's motives differ from contemporary music education, where diversity and inclusion are at the forefront of music education reform. To continue to employ methods in the twenty-first century without a knowledge of the underlying philosophy behind the method is problematic.

In her discussion of "doing philosophy in music education" (Jorgensen, 2006, p. 176), Jorgensen emphasizes the importance of "exposing and evaluating underlying assumptions" (p. 181) of music teaching methods. She argues that within the field of music education, this type of philosophical inquiry of music teaching methods is rarely done. Instead, music teaching approaches are assessed based upon "practical issues rather than the assumptions on which they are based …. Teachers have defended their chosen method(s) on the basis of personally held opinions rather than dispassionately reasoned arguments" (p. 181). Historically, the methods, advocated by MENC and employed by music teachers throughout the United States, like the Orff and Kodály methods, have been evaluated based upon pedagogical efficacy rather than philosophical purpose. Many of the methods and standards which were first recommended in the 1950s continue to be widely used in 2021. The pedagogical goals were explicitly focused on Western classical aesthetics and music.

### Western Classical Musical Superiority

The 1955 source book *Music in American Education* outlined the standards for music teaching from preschool to higher education as well as accreditation and certification criteria. The MENC source books maintained the ideological and pedagogical foundation on which MSNC was founded. For example, *Music in American Education* (1955) reinstated the belief that music education was a "moralizing" and character-building force if "good" music was used, suggesting that "music offers an opportunity to develop moral and spiritual values … Youngsters participating in good music are not likely to be numbered among our juvenile delinquents" (Morgan, 1955, p. 3).

## 72   *Historical Overview*

According to the source book, students who garnered a knowledge of Western classical music, described in the source books as "good" and the "best" music, would become better citizens.

"Much hearing of the best music is raising the standards of taste and appreciation" (Morgan, 1955, p. 5). Western classical music and other Eurocentric artforms, according to the source books, "serve as models of, or guideposts to, what the race recognizes as good" (p. 15), warning that "to be in ignorance of the great products of our culture is to remain a savage" (p. 15). The "taste" and "appreciation" for Western classical music were therefore equated with morality, spirituality, and "good character." Those who lacked this "taste" were simply labeled "savage." The "civilizing" mission and musical saviorism of the eighteenth and nineteenth centuries, therefore, remained a part of music education discourse, even as music education became standardized and codified in the second part of the twentieth century.

The perpetuation of musical saviorism ideology is evident in the source book's description of the music teacher's mission. Music "educators have a matchless opportunity to lead those whom we educate into an experience of discipline, high moral purpose and conduct, and spiritual growth" (Morgan, 1955, p. 8). The music teacher, therefore, with Western classical music and a Western classical music teaching pedagogy, was the missionary in the twentieth-century version of the music "civilizing mission" worthy of, according to the 1955 source book, being "canonized with the saints" and being considered "benefactors of the race" (p. 8).

The MENC source books of the twentieth century perpetuated the ideology of Western classical musical superiority. Towards the end of the twentieth century, even when discussions about multiculturalism and musical diversity were gaining steam, Western classical musical superiority remained, and remains, the ideological backbone of music education because it is ingrained into the assumptions, discourses, and music teaching practices that have been inherited from decades past.

### National Association of Music Education and Equity

In 2020, NAfME re-published their 2000 publication, *Vision 2020: The Housewright Symposium on the Future of Music Education* (Madsen, 2020). The publication documents the discussions that took place at the Housewright Symposium on the Future of Music Education in 1999. The symposium, which brought together 175 music educators, industry representatives, and leaders in the field, focused on articulating the purpose and future of music education. Perhaps it is telling that much of the content in the re-publication remains unchanged. Despite 20 years of demographic, social, educational, and cultural change in the United States, the vision for and of 2020 is largely the same in 2020 as it was in 1999. Rather than use this opportunity to interrogate and problematize that which continues· to be problematic within the field of music education—the systemic and institutional racism, exclusion, and perpetuation of a musical hierarchy which prioritizes a Eurocentric musical epistemology—especially as the global pandemic has reified class and racial inequalities, the 2020 document reinstated the status quo.

Assertions have been made since the Tanglewood symposium (Choate et al., 1967) to diversify and equitize the field, however, systemic change has yet to take place. A field built on assumptions of superiority and saviorism will continue to reinstate and reinstill those assumptions unless a dismantling takes place. The uncritical application of musical concepts, pedagogy, and Eurocentric belief systems about listening and singing will prevent the field from systemic change as will the preservationist agenda and worship of musical "masters." Musical preservation is discussed in the Housewright document (2020):

> Preservation need not be mindless. Our heritage contains monuments of human thought that some call the canon of western civilization, a cultural store that is deemed valuable enough that it ought to be preserved by teaching. Through music study, students gain access to the musical minds of geniuses such as Bach, Mozart, and Beethoven. If music teachers emphasize musical processes that challenge all students to share their musical thoughts—including their musical recreations of the masterworks—through their skills, knowledge and evaluative insights, then music study, even study of the masters, can have a new, stronger focus.
> (Gates, 2020, p. 65)

The assumption that the Western classical canon is the common heritage of American students and teachers demonstrates the Eurocentricity of the field. The suggestion that Western classical music traditions be repackaged to ensure their preservation and relevance is emblematic of the ways in which equity and diversity have been ignored since the Tanglewood symposium in 1967. Rather than reveal and dismantle the practices and discourses that allow for perpetuated exclusion, NAfME has addressed issues of inequity largely by repackaging, re-naming, and redistributing problematic practices and discourses.

This troubled past was, perhaps for the first time, acknowledged in its entirety by Mackie Spradley, NAfME president, in her October 2020 statement. "Given the history of our country, systemic racism is embedded in all facets of our life including education. NAfME, with its 113-year history, is no exception to the impact of racism" (Spradley, 2020, p. 1). Spradley then revealed that, in 2019, NAfME hired an external organization—which specializes in the assessment of institutional unconscious bias—to conduct an assessment of NAfME. The Cook Ross firm produced a *Diversity, Equity, Inclusion, and Access Current State Study* (Cook Ross, 2019) and determined that NAfME's "foundational structure is in fact a barrier to progress in the areas of equity, diversity, inclusion, and access" (Spradley, 2020, p. 1).

## 74  *Historical Overview*

Spradley then called for music educators to recognize "the urgency to respond ... [to] the outcry for equity, diversity, inclusion, and access" (p. 2).

The *Current State Study* provided an assessment of NAfME's institutional culture, organization, and leadership and the ways in which they supported or hindered "diversity, equity, inclusion and access" (Cook Ross, 2019, p. 2). The Cook Ross firm found that many NAfME members view "the lack of visible diversity on NAfME's Board and other prominent leadership positions" in conflict with "NAfME's stated commitment to" diversity and equity (p. 4). The report indicates that "participants ... reported having experienced and overheard racist and sexist remarks, contributing to an organizational culture of exclusion" (p. 4). Participants described the prioritization of band and orchestra as being an archaic focus which "creates defensiveness and tension when other music genres are offered to students or promoted within NAfME" (p. 5). The prioritization of Western classical musical traditions has created what participants described as "an elite culture and worldview that is resistant to change" (p. 5). Music education "Traditions" were reported to be a hindrance to diversity and equity (p. 5). In addition, participants described "historical systems of oppression" (p. 5) within the field of music education that "have prevented diverse musicians, educators and composers from gaining visibility" (p. 5). These systems of exclusion, like "music auditions and competitions," which were described in the report as "inherently biased and exclusionary" (p. 5), have inhibited NAfME's ability to adequately address diversity and equity.

The benefit of having an outside organization well-versed in unconscious and, perhaps, conscious bias, conduct an assessment of an organization deeply steeped in institutional racism and elitism is obvious. Those within the organization who are aware of systemic inequality may have found it hard to articulate or convince others within this organization of these problems. The outside assessment, however, is only beneficial in its analysis of that which *is* and not that which *could be*. The entrenched beliefs—the normalized assumptions of Western classical music and the hierarchy of musical styles, singing styles, and ensembles—are deeply engrained and invisible to those unfamiliar with music education culture. In fact, it is their presumed universality that makes them invisible even to those within the music education field. While the *Current State Study* provided official documentation of that which is problematic within music education, the changes needed to equitize and diversify the field of music education are far more complex and nuanced than can be represented in a neat, quantifiable report. At the end of her address, Spradley (2020) poses the question, "What can we do to eradicate systemic racism and center equity?" (p. 2). While her leadership is providing the impetus for institutional change, changing an organization and educational field whose identity is rooted in the preservation of White supremacism will require a complete overhaul of all that has been presumed and assumed to be true.

## References

Choate, R. A., Fowler, C. B., Brown, C. E., & Wersen, L. G. (1967). The Tanglewood symposium: Music in American society. *Music Educators Journal*, 54(3), 49–80. doi:10.2307/3391187.

Cook Ross. (2019, October). *National Association for Music Education: Diversity, equity, inclusion, & access current state study findings & recommendations report.* https://nafme.org/wp-content/uploads/2020/01/NAfME_DEIA_Executive-Summary_ 2019.pdf.

Damrosch, W., Gartlan, G. H., & Gehrkens, K. W. (1923). *The universal school music series: Teachers book.* Hinds, Hayden & Eldredge.

Downes, O. (1950, December 31). Evangel of music: Violinist. *The New York Times*, 100(33,944).

Gates, T. J. (2020). Why study music? In C. Madsen (Ed.), *Vision 2020: The Housewright Symposium on the future of music education* (pp. 51–76). Rowman & Littlefield.

Glenn, M. (1936). *The world of music: Music activities and practices in kindergarten and elementary grades.* Ginn.

Gregory, B. C. (2016). Educational radio, listening instruction, and the NBC Music Appreciation Hour. *Journal of Radio & Audio Media*, 23(2), 288–305. doi:10.1080/19376529.2016.1224423.

Howe, S. W. (2003). The NBC music appreciation hour: Radio broadcasts of Walter Damrosch, 1928–1942. *Journal of Research in Music Education*, 51(1), 64–77. doi:10.2307/3345649.

Jorgensen, E. R. (2006). On philosophical method. In R. Colwell (Ed.), *MENC handbook of research methodologies* (pp. 176–198). Oxford University Press.

Journal of Proceedings (1921). *Journal of proceedings of the fourteenth annual meeting of the Music Supervisors' National Conference.* Ann Arbor Press.

Kodály, Z. ([1964]1974). *The selected writings of Zoltán Kodály* (L. Halápy & F. Macnicol, Trans.). F. Bónis (Ed.). Boosey & Hawkes.

Koza, J. E. (2008). Listening for whiteness: Hearing racial politics in undergraduate school music. *Philosophy of Music Education Review*, 16(2), 145–155. doi:10.2979/ pme.2008.16.2.145.

Madsen, C. (Ed.). (2020). *Vision 2020: The Housewright symposium on the future of music education.* Rowman & Littlefield.

Mark, M. L. (2008). *A concise history of American music education.* Rowman & Littlefield.

Mark, M. L. (2020). MENC: From Tanglewood to the present. In C. Madsen (Ed.), *Vision 2020: The Housewright Symposium on the future of music education* (pp. 1–18). Rowman & Littlefield.

Martin, G. W. (1983). *The Damrosch dynasty: America's first family of music.* Houghton Mifflin.

Mason, L. W. (1894). *The national music teacher.* Ginn & Co.

Molnar, J. W. (1955). The establishment of the Music Supervisors National Conference, 1907–1910. *Journal of Research in Music Education*, 3(1), 40–50. doi:10.2307/3344410.

Morgan, H. N. (Ed.). (1955). *Music in American Education.* Music Educators National Conference.

## 76   Historical Overview

*Music Supervisors' Bulletin* (1914, September). By our host. *Music Supervisors' Bulletin*, 1(1), 5–6.

NAfME (n.d.). National Association for Music Education. https://nafme.org.

*New York Times* (1946, December 23). Walter Damrosch dies at age of 88. *The New York Times*, 100(33,936), 1.

Orff, C., & Keetman, G. ([1950]1956). *Music for children* (D. Hall & A. Walter, Trans.). B. Schott's Söhne.

Parker, H., McConathy, O., Birge, E. B., & Miessner, W. O. (1918). *Teachers manual for the progressive music series* (vol. 3). Silver, Burdett, & Co.

Perryman, W. R. (1972). *Walter Damrosch: An educational force in American music* (Doctoral dissertation, Indiana University). ProQuest Dissertations Publishing, 7316553.

Ripley, F. H., & Tapper, T. (1895). *Natural course in music*. American Book Co.

Spradley, M. V. (2020, October 8). Statement on upcoming national town hall meetings. https://nafme.org/wp-content/uploads/2020/10/NAfME-Town-Hall-invitation-FINAL.pdf.

Tomlins, W. L. (1919). *The laurel music-reader*. C.C. Birchard & Company.

Tufts, J. W., & Holt, H. E. (1888). *Manual for the use of teachers: To accompany the readers and charts of the Normal Music Course*. Silver, Burdett & Co.

Volk, T. M. (2004). *Music, education, and multiculturalism: Foundations and principles*. Oxford University Press.

# Part III

# Today's Music Classroom

# 7 How Do Our Normalized Practices Impact Children Today?

Drawing from the theoretical discussion in Part I and rooted in the historical analysis of Part II, this chapter provides empirical evidence of the ways in which normalized music teaching practices manifest in today's music classrooms. The purpose of this qualitative case study research was to ascertain the ways in which adolescent music students from diverse, socioeconomically disadvantaged backgrounds perceive the music teaching in their general music classroom.

I used "purposeful sampling" (Creswell, 2013, p. 100) to choose the case for my study. The criteria I used included those about the school at large, student demographics, and age, as well as the teachers' backgrounds. I chose the general music classroom because it is an unelected class and compulsory in this state until sixth grade. I looked for a school in a socioeconomically disadvantaged area with a majority of the student body being Black, Indigenous, People of Color (BIPOC). In addition, the students needed to be in the early stages of adolescence where identity negotiation and formation were salient parts of their lives. Because I was investigating both the general music teaching and the ways in which specific discourses about singing were employed in the general music classroom, the teachers in my study needed to have music education backgrounds with an emphasis on voice. In addition, as a means of better understanding the cultural synchrony of White teachers in primarily non-White contexts, both teachers needed to be White. *Synchrony*, as it relates to culture and communication, is defined by Kim as:

> A state of congruence and harmony in verbal and nonverbal communication patterns of two or more interactants ... [which] occurs when the interactants share common cultural norms and whose psychological orientation toward each other is one of harmony and cooperation.
>
> (Kim, 1992, p. 99)

The school at which this study was conducted is in a Midwestern city in the United States in an area where the poverty level is higher than the national average. Students at this school, from fifth and sixth grade, are primarily BIPOC and from lower socioeconomic backgrounds. The two general music

DOI: 10.4324/9781003099475-10

## 80 Today's Music Classroom

teachers at this school had similar educational backgrounds. Both had Bachelor's and Master's degrees in music education, with an emphasis on voice, from institutions with student bodies that were primarily White. Both teachers were White women in their mid-thirties.

The primary data collection methods consisted of semi-structured, open-ended interviews with students and teachers and field note observations of their music classrooms. Over the course of three months, I conducted 14 semi-structured interviews with students from both classrooms, two teacher interviews, and twice-weekly observations of each classroom. Of the 14 student interviews, seven students were African American, one was from a Honduran immigrant family, one was from a Honduran Mexican immigrant family, one was Latino, one was from an Eritrean immigrant family, and three were European American. The interview data and field notes from the observations were coded, organized, and analyzed into categories and sub-categories using the "constant comparative" method of analysis (Bogdan & Biklen, 2007, p. 73) during data collection and Creswell and Poth's "data-analysis spiral" (2018, pp. 185–187) upon completion of data collection. Although I did not plan to observe two contrasting teaching approaches, the two teachers, Ms. Miller and Ms. Greene, provided me an opportunity to compare a traditional music teaching classroom, where prescriptive Western classical methods were employed, with a non-traditional music classroom that was designed to embrace student autonomy, diversity, and creativity. The field notes and interview data emphasized how these two approaches manifested in substantially different ways with a profound impact.

Descriptions of each student will be woven in with the interview data to provide a richer depiction of each child. In the interviews, the students provided complex and meaningful insight. My hope is to provide a window into each child's world and in doing so honor each of their voices. Pseudonyms for both the teachers and the students will be used throughout.

## What Is Music for These Students?

### Self-expression and Identity

When I asked the students about their favorite music, I was struck by the depth of their responses. Their beliefs about music and the function of music in their lives were complex and emotional. Precious, for example—a precocious, 10-year-old, African American student who sings in her church choir and is the youngest of five girls—connected the text of her favorite song to her oldest sister, their relationship, and her aspirations to be like her sister.

> I like gospel. My favorite song is a church song. In church, there's a song called "I'm a Soldier, in an Army for the Lord," and that's my favorite song. 'Cause when I grow up, I'm going to be a soldier and every time I sing that song at church, I think of me and my future, and I

*Normalized Music Teaching Practices* 81

think of one of my sisters—on the thirty-first on this month, on Halloween, actually, she'll be in the Army for three years. She sometimes, she misses my birthdays because she has drill, and she even misses her birthday 'cause of drill. But she, she always makes up for it, but I don't get mad because it's her job. Sometimes, I … I do get mad, but after a while, I realized that it's her job, like she has to do it.

Tamila, an effervescent, intelligent, and curious fifth grader who was first to invite me to the school festival for pizza and nachos, believed that each person possessed a unique song. She described her own song for me. "My song would be really long. A long note, but … truthful." Tamila lives with her grandparents and brother. She sings church music with her grandparents and her earliest musical memories are of singing gospel music in church. She described the ways in which music can be a form of self-expression.

> There's some songs make you sad, some songs make you happy. And sometimes people like to get emotional and sad. Like if someone gets fired out their job they like to listen to sad songs and just let it all out.

Aisha, an eloquent, 12-year-old African American girl, who lives with her father, openly discussed the ways in which music intersected all aspects of her life and helped her to cope with hardships. As a talented singer and dancer, she used music as a means to express herself. Much like Tamila, Aisha spoke about music being emotionally complex. Both girls described emotionally difficult life events that they had undergone or were currently undergoing. Discussions about music, for Tamila and Aisha, were inextricably linked to the hardships they had faced. For Aisha, singing provided her with an outlet to express some of the emotional turmoil she was experiencing.

> I express myself with singing. Music for me I mean, it just expresses who I am. And music entertains and can get us to start dancing. And music can be just awesome in so many good ways, sad in the same ways, and harsh in the other ways.
>
> Me and my friends, we sing, we write songs together and most of the songs are to me—love. Like that's my topic of songs. Or sometimes they might be scary or sometimes it might be … but my topic really is love.

Kesha, a vibrant, African American, 12-year-old student, also spoke about how she used singing as a form of self-expression and how her vocal identity contributed to her self-esteem. She described her favorite music and the reasons why she chose to express herself with this music.

> Well, um, I think personally that I can sing pretty good. I mean, I'm not the best singer in the world and I'm not the worst, so I think … singing makes me feel more confident. And singing is really fun, and when I

## 82  *Today's Music Classroom*

sing, like if someone says, "Well, she can't sing" well, when I sing it's like I feel I *can* sing.

I sing a lot of Melody Martinez because I'm weird [laughs]. And she's really crazy but I just like her music because she likes to express herself in different ways than other artists. Like, other artists talk about gangs and violence and she will just talk about her childhood and how it was.

### Music and Family

Many of the students' musical preferences and musical identities were interlinked with their families. Kesha recounted a memorable musical moment in her life and the role her family played in her musical confidence.

My first musical experience was in third grade at another school I was going to. My mom had asked me did I want to um, want to sign up for this play we was doing in school, and it was a musical so, I was like, "yeah," so then I had to sing in front of everybody and I was kind of scared at first, but then I seen my mom and my brother in the audience and I was like, "I can do this."

Alma was eager to share about her family's musical traditions. Her parents emigrated from Honduras, bringing with them the rich musical and cultural traditions with which she is surrounded. She made a distinction between the music she learns in music class and her family's musical traditions, which she never had to learn because they are a part of her: "I be dancing and singing bachata with my mom ... Um, I didn't learn it, it's in my blood."

Similarly, Precious described the ways in which music and family were interlinked in her life. She considered music to be an important part of her life and therefore, something about which she was serious. For her, the interlinking of the two demonstrated the importance of each in her life. She said, "I wouldn't do songs just like silly, or something. I'll do something about family, or friends or how much people enjoy being with their family and their friends." Isabella, a warm and grounded 11-year-old girl from a Honduran Mexican immigrant family, described the ways in which music, family, and culture were interconnected in her life.

My dad makes his music by his heart and all his songs have a meaning and while he sings it's kind of like a tradition for our house because my grandpa used to sing, and my grandpa's dad used to sing. So, my dad really likes to sing, and all his brothers and my uncles love to sing too. So, when I listen to music I just like it to be heartful like it has to have meaning, like my dad's.

I connect with my dad's music. I'm not saying there's no meaning here [at school]. Um. My dad is like it has a different meaning and he composes about us and about all the wonderful things and he makes a

*Normalized Music Teaching Practices*  83

different type of music like he puts his heart to it and he writes it in Spanish. He can't speak English that well.

I asked Isabella how she would feel if they sang Spanish and her dad's type of music in music class. She responded emphatically, "I would feel like I'm truly myself because my singing voice is kind of like ... my voice. Um, my voice is ... me! My style."

Destiny, a soft-spoken, African American, 10-year-old girl who was often reprimanded in class, spoke openly and candidly with me about her beliefs about music. She and her mother, grandmother, and aunt share a passion for singing and Beyoncé's singing in particular, although she mentioned that her grandmother prefers to listen to "old school music." Music plays a salient role in Destiny's relationship with her grandmother. As one of four children, with younger twin sisters and an older brother, Destiny's grandmother has played an important role in her upbringing. Her earliest musical memory, as well as other musical memories, included her family. She recounted, "Sometimes, when I was like three or four, my grandma used to read bed stories to me, they used to have singing in it. She used to sing to me that was inside the book. The song that was inside of the books."

hroughout my conversations with the students, I found that the discussion about music, for many of them, was inextricably linked to discussions about family and culture. This was the case whether they favored their family's music, like Alma, Isabella, and others, or whether, like Mercy, they preferred popular music. Mercy said, "I like to listen to hip-hop and pop music. My family listens to religious music. They listen to music from Eritrea, because they were born in Africa."

Davion, a gentle-natured, passionate, African American, 11-year-old boy, shared his family's passion for rap, however, when it came to the subjects about which he rapped, he did not include his family.

EMILY: What, is your favorite music?
DAVION: Rap.
EMILY: What about your family?
DAVION: Rap. Me and my stepdad.
EMILY: What type of things do you like to rap about?
DAVION: Um, everything ... But everything that I know.
EMILY: Can you give me some examples?
DAVION: Like money.
EMILY: Like what about money?
DAVION: Like what you, what you could do with it.
EMILY: Can you give me an example of what you could do with it?
DAVION: Spend it. Save it.
EMILY: Would you ever talk about your family in your rap?
DAVION: No.

84  *Today's Music Classroom*

EMILY: What's the most important thing to you about your family?
DAVION: Them being alive.

The conversation I had with Davion was indicative of his soft spoken, to-the-point manner of holding conversations. Yet, with just a few words, he was able to convey the complexities of his reality and a mature awareness about life's indeterminacy.

This was a common occurrence throughout my conversations with the students. As we spoke about what one might assume to be a seemingly uncontroversial topic for adolescents of this age, the complexities of the students' lives made their way into the discussion about music. Although I was hesitant to pursue topics that seemed psychologically outside of the realm of this study and my expertise, I realized that the very grown-up realities of these young students intersected all aspects of their lives. Music seemed to provide a powerful and positive way of negotiating these complexities.

Matt, a shy, small in stature, and quiet, European American, shared his family's passion for country music. Without me asking why he shared this passion, he explained how he had to stay in the hospital for three weeks after birth due to complications. He links the singing of country music to his family's celebration of his discharge from the hospital.

> I like country like my mom, my sister, and my grandma. Once I turned three weeks old my mom and my family were singing country around me—because I came home from the doctors.

Much like Davion and Matt, Sarah described complexities in her life through her discussions about music and family. Sarah, a sweet and introspective girl with thick bottle-cap glasses and long blonde hair, came to our interview with large holes in the knees of her tights and stains on her clothes. This did not faze her, as she was excited to share her thoughts on singing and music. She exuded a pure love for singing and for learning new musical instruments. She talked about how her father had a band and was teaching her multiple instruments. Her struggle with ADHD and the ways in which her father helped her made their way into the conversation about music.

> Um, I'm, I'm not very picky with music, but my favorite is country ... my grandfather likes country as well ... My dad likes metal; he's a drummer and has a band. His band comes over to practice. My dad is teaching me how to play guitar. It's very hard for me to play because I'm ADHD so it's hard to focus both things at once. I can strum right now but it's very hard for me to do the fingers and ... So, my dad's teaching me.

# References

Bogdan, R. C., & Biklen, S. K. (2007). *Qualitative research for education: An introduction to theories and methods* (5th ed.). Pearson/Allyn and Bacon.

Creswell, J. W. (2013). *Qualitative inquiry and research design: Choosing among five approaches* (3rd ed.). Sage Publications.

Creswell, J. W., & Poth, C. (2018). *Qualitative inquiry & research resign* (4th ed.). Sage Publications.

Kim, Y. Y. (1992). Synchrony and intercultural communication. In D. Crookall, & K. Arai (Eds.), *Global interdependence: Simulation and gaming perspectives proceedings of the 22nd International Conference of the International Simulation and Gaming Association* (pp. 99–105). Springer-Verlag. doi:10.1007/978-4-431-68189-2_11.

# 8 Two Music Teaching Approaches

The two teachers in this study taught with contrasting music teaching approaches. One teacher employed a traditional music teaching approach with Western classical music methods and the other a non-traditional music teaching approach designed to embrace student autonomy, diversity, and creativity. The field notes and interview data emphasized the ways in which these two approaches manifested in substantially different ways with a profound impact. In this chapter, findings from interviews with teachers and students are discussed as a means of shedding light on culturally sustaining music teaching.

## Traditional Music Teaching Approach

The teaching of the first teacher, Ms. Greene, incorporated common music teaching methods, traditional expectations of music students, and normalized beliefs about what was "appropriate" and "good" musical and non-musical behavior. Ms. Greene's teaching, based primarily on her continuing Orff training and her music teacher education, was emblematic of traditional, Western Classical-centric music education in the United States.

### Disciplining and Silencing of Bodies and Voices

The students described Ms. Greene's fifth-grade class as a strict environment where they are frequently disciplined. When I asked Kesha why she thought they were always getting into trouble, she responded:

> 'Cuz they didn't like what they were doing. She never switched up what we were doing. We were always doing the same thing every day. All we did was sing the same songs and we just looked at the board and said like "ti ti ta" and stuff …. And then everybody would just be disrespectful to her and … talk back and stuff. And she would just … she would just call the principal.

Kesha connected discipline, student interest, and student behavior. She suggested that student misbehavior was caused by a lack of interest in the

DOI: 10.4324/9781003099475-11

Two Music Teaching Approaches  87

content being taught. My field notes reflected a similar sentiment as those expressed by Kesha. Class activities did not engage the students' interest. The amount of time spent on discipline, and the little time spent on music activities which may have been more relevant for the students, contributed to increasing student disengagement and disinterest. The mismatch between Ms. Greene's expectations and the students' expectations, the main reason for student and teacher frustration, seemed to be largely curricular.

The students described a disconnect between music at home and music at school. Alma noted, "well, in music class and ... Home, it's like a different culture." Similarly, Isabella stated, "In my house the song is more like love, family, and things like that. But my house I don't know how to explain it but it's really different [from school]." Other students who described an incongruence between the music at home and the music in school could hardly imagine having their home music at school. Mercy, a bright, well-spoken, 11-year-old girl from an Eritrean immigrant family, described her musical experience outside of school: "I'm in the church choir with my friends. It's like Christian music that we do for Jesus and all the things from the Bible. We use drums to help us keeping the beat." When I asked her how she would feel if she sang that music in music class, she responded, "I would feel kind of weird because it's in a different language. What I sing is in a different language, so yeah." Like Mercy, Precious seemed to have never considered singing music that was relevant for her in music class:

I mean, it'll kind of be different from the songs from like the normal songs we sing [in music class], 'cause it kind of like, it kind of has a beat a little bit, but I still would not mind singing it in music class.

Throughout my field notes, I often took note of restless energy and the lack of movement in Ms. Greene's class. I was impressed with how well the students could perform the rhythmic activities. For many of them, I wrote, "their whole bodies seemed to yearn to dance when they clapped the rhythmic patterns or repeated the body percussion sequence," although the clapping patterns and strictly choreographed body percussion allowed little room for extra movement. Luis, a thin, lanky, soft-spoken, 12-year-old boy with Latino heritage, reflected on his experience in Ms. Greene's music class. A particularly salient point he and others made, one that I also often took note of in my field notes, was a lack of opportunity for movement which, in turn, created more student restlessness.

In Ms. Greene's class, we would just, like, sit. I mean, we would move, but like ... Not like we do in this class [Ms. Miller's]. Most of the time we'd just get like, rhythm sticks, and then that's all we would do.

One example from my field notes was when "the students stood and did body percussion. Ms. Greene had them sit after two minutes. They seemed

## 88  Today's Music Classroom

frustrated that they had to sit again." When I asked Ms. Greene about how she chooses her curriculum, she said, "I write it all myself. I go to Orff workshops." I asked her if she found that her students' interests changed from school to school. She responded:

> Definitely different interests. I still do the same things I did at the private catholic school. The fifth graders at the private catholic school seemed a little more innocent than here. Here, if they don't like something they have no problem expressing it.

I then asked Ms. Greene about the Orff philosophy. She said, "involve the child as much as you can with speech, body percussion, instruments." She asserted that it has helped her immensely in her teaching. Although Ms. Greene used body percussion and instruments, based upon the students' perceptions and my field notes, there was a disconnect between what Ms. Greene thought was relevant for the students and what actually was relevant.

### Strict Vocal Approach—Western Classical Style

In addition to strict classroom discipline, the students perceived the singing in Ms. Greene's classroom as one in which their bodies and voices were strictly disciplined. In my notes, I frequently quoted Ms. Greene's language about posture and body containment: "Hands down, touch your legs … singing posture, sitting on pockets, legs are down flat, back is nice and straight and tall." Additionally, I noted how shocked I was at the way students were required to enter the hallway from the music classroom: "each student's arms were crossed tightly across his chest, his chin was to be tucked, eyes lowered, mouths closed." None of the singing activities were rhythmic and they mostly involved the head voice. The students perceived Ms. Greene's vocal approach to be strict based on the focus on head voice and the emphasis on proper singing posture and mouth position. The fixed posture allowed little opportunity for body movement while singing. The students perceived this as a disciplining of their voices.

For Aisha, the disciplining of her voice translated as a disciplining of her own person. She said, "But before in Ms. Greene's class, I mean, it was just strict. Like, straight up strict—right posture, and all that stuff." She went on to say,

> It seemed like if I was to be myself, I'd be wrong. That was a problem. So, I didn't really do everything, like … I was that one kid that really deliberately did everything the opposite of what she said. Like, Ms. Greene, because she'd say like "sing with a golf ball in your mouth" like "oh."

Kesha attributed the fear of singing that many of the students experienced in class to the strict vocal teaching: "I think they're scared that they're gonna be like, 'Oh, he can't sing' or 'Oh, she can't sing.' Because they're scared that the teacher will be like, 'Well, you don't sing good enough for this class.'" I asked Kesha to describe the vocal teaching. She said, "She would tell us to like, sing with a golf, like we had a golf ball in our mouth, and we'd have to sit up straight and work on good singing posture." I then asked Kesha how this teaching influenced the singing. She responded, "It made singing less fun and it made us like, I was second guessing if I wanted to be in choir this year."

Many of the students expressed a dislike for the type of singing in Ms. Greene's class and emphasized the strict posture and mouth shape. Others recognized the ways in which the singing was different from the ways they sang outside of school. When I asked Mercy how she would describe the singing in music class, she responded, "It's pretty different to the singing at home. The music at home is more upbeat and it's easier to dance to. The one in Miss Greene's, it's more just to listen to. You can't really dance to it." Many students described the singing in music class as devoid of body movement and for many of the students, like Mercy, whose family is Eritrean, singing without body movement was foreign. The primary focus on the head voice was also noted by students as an aspect of the classroom singing experience that was different from singing at home. Precious compared the singing in music class with her church choir singing: "The music class is kind of higher." Isabella offered a similar observation when I asked her to compare the singing in music class with the singing she did with her family at home: "Well, it's really different because right here [music class] we do like a lot of high pitch things." The students perceived the singing in Ms. Greene's class as higher based upon the primary use of the head voice. In my field notes I wrote that Ms. Greene asked for a "nice pretty sound," which consisted of, based upon my observations, the use of pure head voice. I never heard her use a mixed sound or chest voice. Although the pitch range was appropriate for the students, they perceived the singing to be much higher because of the head voice vocal register.

### Vocal Inhibition

Because of the strict vocal approach, I found that students were hesitant to sing, even if they had strong vocal models at home. Matt described his voice at home and in music class as two different voices. In music class, he said his voice was "not that loud and whenever I sing I go behind something because I don't want to get seen singing. I was always shy singing." At home, Matt sings country with his mom. When I asked him who he hears singing the most in his life, he said, "My mom. She sings country and sometimes I listen but most of the time I sing with her." When I asked him how he sang with his mom, he replied, "Just normally. Not soft or anything."

When I asked Precious, a confident and spunky fifth grader, whom she hears singing the most in her life, she replied, "um, me." As an active

90  *Today's Music Classroom*

participant in the music ministry at her church and in a local children's choir, she expressed confidence in her singing voice. I asked her to describe her own singing voice, to which she replied, "Um, it kind of depends because sometimes if I'm like really happy, I sing super high, super loud, and super long. And if I'm kind of like sad, I kind of sing like soft sometimes." I then asked her to describe her singing voice in Ms. Greene's music class. She said it was:

> Just the way that it's supposed to be sung. If it's supposed to be like sung high, then high. Low, then low. Not loud. Not like, [demonstrates] dah-dah-dah-dah-dah [loud and smiling]. I mean not too loud, not to the point where I can hear myself loud.

Although Precious did not express hesitation to sing in music class, like Matt, she clearly delineated between the singing that took place in music class and the rest of the singing in her life.

Similarly, Tamila, Mercy, Isabella, and Alma described rich singing experiences with which they were involved outside of school. Although they felt confident to sing in those settings, they felt inhibited to sing in music class. Tamila, who actively participated in church music with her grandparents, and whose first musical memory was from church, described how she sang in music class. She said, "I never really sing with my real voice." When I asked her why she thought she did not use her real voice in music class, she replied, "I don't want anyone really to hear my voice." Mercy also felt confident when she sang in church and described her dad as a strong vocal model. When I asked her if she liked to sing she said, "It's really easy for me to sing stuff." However, when I asked her how she felt when she sang in music class, she quickly responded, "Yeah, well I don't like to sing in front of other people because I get shy easily."

Similarly, my multiple discussions with Isabella revealed her love of singing with her family and, as mentioned before, when I asked her how she would feel if she were to sing Spanish and her dad's type of music in music class, she said, "I would feel like I'm truly myself because my singing voice is kind of like … my voice. Um, my voice is … me! My style." However, when I asked her how she feels when she sings in music class, her response was, "Hm. Like I'm kind of like the shy person when I sing it's just like I get nervous [laughs]!" The confidence with which Alma described her rich tradition of singing and dancing with her family did not carry over into the music classroom. When I asked her to describe her own singing in the music classroom, she said, "I'm shy. I'd sing …. But when I would sing, my face was red."

### Implications of Traditional Music Teaching Approach

The students' negative descriptions of Ms. Greene's music class, coupled with Ms. Greene's expressions of frustration, illuminated the cultural incongruence between Ms. Greene and her students. By traditional university music standards, Ms. Greene is an excellent musician and music teacher. She has a thorough understanding of Western classical music education methods, the Orff method, and Western classical vocal pedagogy. In the same vein, the students' perceptiveness, rich musical backgrounds, and authenticity became apparent to me in our interviews. Ms. Greene's commitment to teaching music in the ways she was trained to teach led to a music classroom in which the students felt silenced and she felt out of control.

The diverse students in the traditional music classroom perceived this classroom as a strict environment where their bodies and voices were disciplined. For many, the disciplining of their bodies and voices meant that they could not be themselves in the music classroom. The silencing of the students' identities led them to react either by retreating or by deliberately misbehaving. Those who misbehaved were more strictly disciplined, which allowed for a perpetual cycle of silencing, reacting, and discipline. Students who responded to the strict classroom culture by retreating were inhibited in their musical expression and exploration.

The traditional teacher's musical epistemology informed her approach in the music classroom. The Eurocentric emphasis on objectification produced an "ontological distance" (Domínguez, 2017, p. 228) between the teacher and her students, making it difficult for her to empathically engage with her students. The lack of understanding of students' musical epistemologies led the teacher to indiscriminately employ prescriptive musical methods, thereby alienating her students and herself from meaningful music-making and stripping them of musical agency.

## Non-Traditional Music Teaching Approach

### Student Agency and Musical Autonomy

Like Ms. Greene, Ms. Miller, a White woman in her mid-thirties, has Bachelor's and Master's degrees in music education with a vocal emphasis, as well as Orff certification. During my first observation of Ms. Miller's class, I immediately observed a different educational approach. I noted in my field notes that "students were eager to learn, volunteered frequently and seemed to be having fun." I noted that Ms. Miller seemed to have great rapport with the students. She spoke physically close to them. I wrote, "Ms. Miller talks to them close by, like friends. There is no distinct line between the students and her." She communicated with her students in a manner that was familiar to them and allowed for a respectful banter between herself and the students to take place during classroom instruction. The first thing I noticed about Ms. Miller's speaking voice was her use of African American Vernacular English (AAVE) with which her students were familiar. Although she is a White woman, the use of AAVE seemed natural and was well received by the students. Her singing style was primarily a mixed voice

## 92 *Today's Music Classroom*

with belting. I never heard her use pure head voice. As I listened to the recordings of her classes, I noted that her speaking tone was conversational and warm.

During every observation, I wrote in my field notes that this class is a great example of "flow" (Csikszentmihalyi, 1993).[1] Students were engaged, activities were well-paced, and she provided a lot of variety. While listening to music, students were given the freedom to sit around the room, on chairs, risers, or on the floor. A few students would walk around the room during a listening activity; some tried the Samba dance steps, others felt the music. In my field notes I wrote, "Ms. Miller is relaxed when kids are jumping around—not such a 'disciplinarian.'"

During one class session, Ms. Miller had the students listen to a piece of music and then write on the multiple white boards around the room what they heard. One student wrote, "wood block thingy," to which Ms. Miller responded, "very descriptive, I like it." During many of my observations, I noted that students were given opportunities to compose and improvise. Ms. Miller would often say, "You have the freedom to mess around with this a bit." During one class session, they composed a piece as a class. As they were finishing the end of the composition, Ms. Miller asked students to write their ideas on the white boards. Some of the responses were: "Embellish end … A big boom … The way we came in … We should fade out and get quiet as we do it … We should slow down at the end." The class tried all of the suggestions and discussed how they would finish the piece.

### A Typical Day

Ms. Miller's classes combined elements of composition, improvisation, listening, dance, singing, and instrument-playing, with each unit structured around a particular musical culture and musical style. She began each unit with an overview of the historical and social context of each musical culture to provide a frame of reference for students' musical exploration. With each subsequent class, students explored with more depth the socio-historical and cultural underpinnings of the music. One example, the Brazilian *Embolada*, historically influenced by both African American rap and African musical elements, sparked a rich discussion and catalyzed students' interest in the historical and cultural background of the musical form.

Once students had a preliminary understanding of the musical context, they began their musical, compositional, and improvisational exploration of the musical style. In small groups, students composed Brazilian *Emboladas*, drawing from their own musical interests and backgrounds. Musical exploration sparked further discussions about the music's cultural and historical context and the ways in which musical forms can draw from multiple musical cultures and influences. Students engaged with the musical form both in musical and non-musical ways, which allowed them to more deeply engage with the music. When Davion discovered the ways in which the

Brazilian *Embolada* was influenced by African American rap, he was able to more fully connect with the musical form. His group's *Embolada* composition incorporated rap within the *Embolada* form and style. For Aisha's group, the *Embolada* composition project allowed her to incorporate her interests in choreography and singing into a new musical framework. In my field notes, I wrote, "students are all eager to go first, to perform their *Embolada* compositions for their peers. No one is inhibited."

Subsequent classes within the Brazilian unit explored other Brazilian musical forms. During one class, Ms. Miller introduced the Brazilian *Samba*. After describing the historical and cultural framework for the musical form, Ms. Miller played a recording of Brazilian *Samba*. In my field notes I wrote, "while listening, students are moving, feeling the music, smiling, with energy." After listening, Ms. Miller asked them to write on the board what they heard. After listening and writing on the board, Ms. Miller had the students try the *Samba* dance steps. Immediately from dancing she moved to the next activity, which was watching a 1940s Disney video clip with *Samba*. Ms. Miller asked them to "notice anything the same or different." Students watched the video from various places in the room. Some reclined on the risers in the back of the room, others lay down on the carpet; a few sat in the chairs while others sat against the wall in the back corner of the room. After watching the video and discussing the similarities and differences, Ms. Miller asked the students to return to their chairs for instructions. A few minutes later, the students were out of their chairs choosing drums for the next activity. With a variety of drums, the students sat on the floor with Ms. Miller and took part in an interactive video lesson on *Samba* drumming. The interactive video lesson, projected onto the large screen at the front of the classroom, provided step-by-step instructions from an accomplished Brazilian drummer. His lesson explored multiple rhythms and drumming patterns that were relevant for the *Samba* musical style. Both Ms. Miller and her students took part in the lesson. I noted in my field notes that "all the students were engaged and eager to try the patterns." After the video lesson, Ms. Miller asked her students which rhythms were the most difficult. They discussed what they had learned. Following the discussion, Ms. Miller had the students try the *Samba* dance steps to the specific drumming patterns they had learned. Ms. Miller explored each musical unit creatively and drew from a wide range of diverse sources so as to best engage her students. When the musical unit required skills beyond her expertise, she incorporated video lessons and other musical resources.

### Curriculum

In my observations, I noticed that students had a lot of autonomy as well as the opportunity to move. When I asked Ms. Miller to describe the ways in which she plans the class, this was her response:

94  *Today's Music Classroom*

Well, um, you know, I asked them about countries. Like what countries would you be interested in learning about? Some of them would go look at the map. And then we listed, and they just listed a bunch. You know? So, I have a, a spreadsheet I think for both the classes on the countries that they listed. And even right now, I mean we've done Brazil and Greece. And I mean, it's you know, November! But, um, but just because we've been able to kind of expand and do some of that stuff. And just because they got so into creating [laugh] …

So, I'm like, "Wow, you can do this. It's worth it." And then, you know, listening to the other stuff, and I think, too, just letting them, I mean, they have to sit in the class all the time too. And so, um, letting them have some freedom to create their own thing within those parameters has been pretty interesting. Um, and they, they like doing that. So, I mean, that's boring stuff where I'm kind of talking to you and I'm giving you the information. But when we are learning something altogether, letting them be creative kind of on their own or come up with stuff too, I think has helped.

I also asked Ms. Miller whether she currently uses, or has used in the past, her Orff training in the classroom.

Um, yeah. I mean, since I've had the training, used some of it. It, it's kind of dependent. I've done a lot of like movement stuff, you know, from that aspect of … And then there's still the improvisation aspect. Or composing. So, I guess it's been, it's kind of dependent on year to year.

Interestingly, Ms. Miller compared the ways in which Ms. Greene uses Orff in the classroom with her own approach.

I don't, um, you know, Ms. Greene is pretty strictly Orff. And is able, you know, I mean, and she has, she has been able to do that. And for me, I don't necessarily, I don't ever necessarily just use that curriculum.

In addition, one of Ms. Miller's reasons for not using a strictly Orff method was because of her approach to singing. She said, "But like being a singer too, like there's, you know, other folk songs and things that I want to bring into it. So, I don't say that I'm just always that [Orff]."

When I spoke with Ms. Miller's students, I was struck by how much their perceptions were in line with hers. They spoke about the aspects of her class that were most meaningful for them, which included autonomy, self-expression, active music-making, and movement. Aisha, the student who "deliberately did everything the opposite of what [Ms. Greene] said," noted that Ms. Miller's class provided her with the opportunity for self-expression.

Two Music Teaching Approaches  95

Because it's free. Especially with this assignment because I like to express what I have. It's awesome because the singing here—we're learning about other cultures. I love like going to other countries like and learning about what they do because I want to go out of my comfort zone to other countries to see what they do, and then bring it back.

Aisha emphasized that she felt free to be herself and felt respected by Ms. Miller: "It's not really the class itself, it's the teacher. Like I like Ms. Miller really because she's open. She's free, I mean, like I said, she's not strict. She's just like a real person with us."

Davion expressed what he liked about Ms. Miller's class: "I like the creativity. Like, we get to pick our own songs and stuff." When I asked Davion what he would change about the class, he said he would not change one thing. Luis and Kesha both appreciated the ways in which they could be active in the class, both physically through movement and as active music-makers.

My favorite thing is that we don't have to just sit down and listen to a teacher talk. We get to get up and get active and um, we get to make our own songs, and we don't have to stick to the same topic all the time. Like if you want to go to a different country or another state or something where you can learn their music and then you won't feel like, well, I know nothing about this place at all.

I have multiple field notes that detail the ways in which movement in Ms. Miller's class seemed to dispel the need for "classroom management." For Luis, in particular, the opportunity to move in class helped him to focus.

I like this class. It's not like any other class. This is like the time where I just get that energy up, and it's like …. We don't just sit and learn stuff, we dance around and … we do a lot of stuff.

When I spoke with Ms. Miller about teaching challenges, she never mentioned discipline or classroom management. Instead, she spoke about inconsistency being her biggest teaching challenge. Interestingly, she was most challenged by the lack of consistency amongst teachers and with curriculum rather than by student behavior.

### Description of Vocal Teaching

During my observations, as noted earlier, I was impressed with the ways in which Ms. Miller used her vocality, both in speaking and in singing, in ways that were relevant for the students. She spoke with the students in ways that were familiar to them, both in dialect and subject matter. Most of the students were unable to articulate the ways in which her singing compared to their family members', but when I asked Jayla, an articulate, confident,

## 96 *Today's Music Classroom*

African American, 11-year-old girl, how Ms. Miller's singing compared to the Gospel singing with which she was familiar, she emphatically declared, "She *sings* Gospel music! She sings music and sometimes she'll be singing it ... she'll be singing Gospel... pretty much sing ... well pretty much sing anything, all types of music that doesn't have cusses."

Jayla had spoken at length about her mother's traditional gospel singing when I asked her to describe music that was meaningful for her. When I asked her how Ms. Miller's voice compared to her mother's voice, she said "They sound exactly— ... no ... Ms. Miller has more experience than my mom." I was impressed that she thought Ms. Miller's voice and her mother's voices were so similar. She seemed reluctant to say "exactly" so as not to be disrespectful of Ms. Miller's experience.

### Vocal Empowerment

A majority of students in Ms. Miller's classroom, regardless of whether they had vocal models at home, had positive vocal esteem. Kesha was one of the few who had family members at home who liked to sing. When I asked her if her mom liked to sing, she responded, "Yes. She went to karaoke last night!" Kesha spoke about how she did a lot of singing at home with both her mom and her sister. When I asked her whether she was confident singing in front of people, she responded by saying, "I was singing on the bus this morning." Kesha's vocal esteem appeared to be influenced positively by vocal models at home—her mom and sister—and in her music classroom—Ms. Miller.

Luis, on the other hand, did not have parents or family members at home with whom he sang. He said, "I don't usually sing." When I asked him if his parents sang to him or if he heard them sing, he replied, "No. My mom doesn't sing." Despite not singing at home, Luis said, "I feel happy when I sing in here [Ms. Miller's class] ... Uh ... I like this class." Like Luis, Aisha did not have a vocal model at home. She lived with her single father and had not seen her mother in two years. When I asked her whether her father liked to sing, she responded bluntly, "He doesn't like to sing." I was surprised to hear this because Aisha appeared to be confident when she sang in class. She was the soloist in the group presentations I observed and was eager to sing for me in our interview. She also described a performing group she was in the process of starting with the support and help of Ms. Miller.

> Me, my friends and some other people, there's 12 people that know about this group I'm trying to start called "WGT." It's uh, stands for "we got talent." And so, what it basically is like singing, dancing, acting and it's for people that didn't get to do stuff they wanted to. And so, my group allows them to do whatever they want and perform it and do stuff like that.

Despite not having family members with whom they sang, Luis and Aisha were both positively influenced by their vocal model at school.

When I spoke with Davion about singing, he assured me that he did not like to sing at home or at school despite the fact that he enjoyed Ms. Miller's class. Although Davion admitted he did not like to sing, I heard him confidently rap in front of the class many times, oftentimes with melodic content and always with vocal inflection. He also insisted on rapping for me in our interview. Throughout my observations of Ms. Miller's class, I was consistently impressed with the students' vocal confidence as they sang in front of each other and for the teacher.

### Culturally Sustaining Music Teaching

Students were empowered to express themselves freely and authentically in Ms. Miller's non-traditional music classroom. This freedom manifested in uninhibited body entrainment and free vocal expression. In addition to musical embodiment, students valued the freedom of creativity in composition and interpretation. They emphasized how they were free to be themselves in this class. Many of them recognized that this freedom was because of the ways in which the teacher respected and cared for them and treated them as "people." In addition, the teacher's ability to sing the styles of music that were meaningful for her students communicated to them that she valued their musical cultures. Her attention to speaking and the dialect and nuanced communication styles of her students empowered her students and nurtured their vocal confidence.

By attending to her students' musical epistemologies with care and respect, the non-traditional teacher in this study enacted culturally sustaining music teaching. The vocal-esteem of many of the students had been harmed by traditional music teaching. A few students had begun to retreat and had been too inhibited to sing. A few had reacted defiantly to the traditional music teaching and had been strictly disciplined. The non-traditional music classroom culture, however, provided an environment in which the students' identities could be reaffirmed and their musical spirits could heal. The teacher's attention to students' musical epistemologies empowered her students to be agents of their own musical expression and to more fully be themselves in the music classroom.

### Note

1 The eight "characteristic dimensions of the flow experience," include: "1) clear goals; 2) personal skills are well suited to given challenges; 3) action and awareness merge; 4) irrelevant stimuli disappear from consciousness, worries and concerns are temporarily suspended; 5) a sense of potential control; 6) loss of self-consciousness ... a sense of growth and of being part of some greater entity; 7) altered sense of time, which usually seems to pass faster; and 8) what one does becomes autotelic, or worth doing for its own sake" (Csikszentmihalyi, 1993, pp. 178–179).

## References

Csikszentmihalyi, M. (1993). *The evolving self: A psychology for the third millennium*. HarperCollins.

Domínguez, M. (2017). "Se hace puentes al andar:" Decolonial teacher education as a needed bridge to culturally sustaining and revitalizing pedagogies. In D. Paris & H. S. Alim (Eds.), *Culturally sustaining pedagogies: Teaching and learning for justice in a changing world* (pp. 225–245). Teachers College Press.

# 9 How Do Students Describe a Meaningful Music Classroom?

## Students Value Cultural Plurality

In the interviews, the students articulated their visions of a meaningful music classroom. Their descriptions of a meaningful music learning experience shed light on the ways in which music teaching can be culturally sustaining and affirming. The students communicated that they, themselves, value cultural plurality. They value their own music as well as the music of their peers. A meaningful classroom, for them, is one in which all students' voices and interests are recognized. When I asked Tamila how she would teach music, if she were the teacher, she had constructive and explicit directions for me:

> Well first you start off introducing yourself. Say your name and what you like to do. And then you go around like in a circle saying what they like to do and stuff. And like what's their favorite beat, what they like to sing and stuff, like what you're doing to me right now, but don't take this long because you got to get to everyone.

Throughout my interviews, I was impressed by the ways in which the students articulated the need for diversity in the music classroom. This included music that was meaningful for them, their peers, as well as music from other cultures. If he were the teacher, Davion said, "I would do a little bit of everything. Like, some rap one day. Um, maybe like, go around the world and do like different songs." When I asked Davion why he thought kids should take music class, he responded, "cultural reasons, instead of just sitting down and writing it on paper, learning about it." Similarly, Jayla and Aisha described what their classrooms would be like, if they were the music teacher.

> Everybody can do what their favorite music is, like rap ... like we could learn stuff in Africa and everything there, except I would choose somebody to like instead of me choosing them, I would probably let them have a little bit more freedom.
>
> (Jayla)

DOI: 10.4324/9781003099475-12

100　*Today's Music Classroom*

I would say, um, you know, do what Ms. Miller does. Go to different countries, do all that and you know just try to see what the students like instead of what you think is best. What you think is right. I mean, it's always good to ask, have more than one idea for yourself and when the class comes, share your ideas with those, see which ones they like and see what they want to do.

(Aisha)

In their interviews, both Precious and Isabella, at separate points, discussed ways in which a music teacher could incorporate each student's voice to form a collective sound. Precious suggested:

Um, I think I might let the kids write their own songs, and I'd take different sections of the song and turn it into one big song. So, each person has their own point, and how they like to do it in their own mind.

Isabella had a similar suggestion:

When we sing altogether and when we start singing like a harmony, I like how all the different voices connect together and make a new sound. I like music like when it's different and we pitch in everyone's ideas like I would like if I was the teacher, I would sit everyone in a circle and I would pick each one person to pick a style they like. So, we can compose a song we all like and it's everyone's style.

Isabella emphasized joy. She said, "If I could change music at school or a different type of school. I would make it more joyful and meaningful and we would all sing it together." In addition, she also emphasized the importance of using music that is meaningful for the students: "So, I would make it like a harmony like we're happy all together and like that and I would like kids to listen to music that touches their heart and helps them understand lessons about life."

## Students Value Autonomy

When I asked Jayla, if she were the music teacher, whether singing would be important for her, she replied, "It depends on what type of singing or if somebody wants to actually do the singing?" I then asked her what type of singing she thought was important for music teaching. She responded, "Um, anything that they choose. They get to choose. Well, they equally have to vote, and if they get mad at me, that's a 'them' problem, not a 'me' problem." In addition to autonomy being important for Jayla, she also talked about the ways in which the students can teach the teacher, if the music is unfamiliar.

Each vote obviously always going to be something that they know, I'd say, I don't know none of this music—you all teach me … because if somebody in the class wants to um ... wants to ... wants to be a music teacher, they have their chance to be a teacher. ... Like, I'd say, you teach me the lyrics.

Kesha and Mercy also expressed the importance of autonomy and repertoire as a means of garnering student interest. Mercy suggested, "You should listen to everybody's ideas and have a vote to see which ones should be better and which ones you should use. Ideas for what kind of music to do and what kind of notes to use." Kesha advised that teachers should "make sure to aks your students what they want to do too because if they're not interested then they're not going to do anything."

## Students Value the Opportunity to Express Themselves

In addition to the importance of cultural plurality and autonomy, the students expressed the importance of composition and creativity. They valued the opportunity to express themselves and to be imaginative and creative. Mercy suggested:

> What I don't like is that sometimes I just want some free time on the instruments. We don't really get that. For half of the time, I would do something together and we have to work on something. The other half of the time, I would help them out with things and I would give them free time to explore.

Throughout all my discussions with Davion, he reiterated how much he valued the opportunity to compose and be creative. He suggested, "Maybe like have them make their own songs. Maybe like give them like, like ... when class is almost over maybe give them a little bit of free time to add some creativity."

## Encouragement Over Discipline

As part of the discussion about a meaningful music classroom, students expressed the need for encouragement, particularly when it came to singing confidence. Kesha suggested:

> Well, I think the teacher who thinks that one of their students is not confident; if they want to help them get more confidence, they could like tell them "You sing good" ... and "I think you should try harder" and just give them good encouraging words.

In addition to encouragement, many students discussed the ways in which a strict environment negatively impacted their confidence. As mentioned earlier, Aisha admitted that in Ms. Greene's class she "was that one kid that

## 102 *Today's Music Classroom*

really deliberately did everything the opposite of what she said" in reaction to the strict environment. When I observed Aisha in Ms. Miller's class, she was a leader and a positive influence on her peers. She attributed the change in her character in music class to a less strict and more positive environment.

> And then um, for being a teacher, just I mean, try to be positive. Don't bring up every negative thing that's ever happened. I mean, if that student or somebody is being disrespectful or something, hit 'em back with kindness. I mean they will probably do the same thing back.

Similarly, Precious described a music class environment which would be meaningful for her: "Let them have fun while they're singing. Let them be, let them have a big smile on their face or do a little dance around. Just let them be happy, be free."

### More Singing (Low and Fast)

When I asked Ms. Greene how much singing is typically done in Orff, she replied, "I think it depends on the teacher and the kids. There are some Orff teachers that don't really ever sing with their kids and there are some that sing even more than I do." She went on to explain that "the fifth grade this year, kind of had the attitude that they don't want to sing." Despite Ms. Greene's assertion that her students, in her words, "had the attitude that they don't want to sing," my discussions with her students revealed that they in fact wanted to sing more. It seemed to them that they did very little singing in class. For example, when I asked Sarah what she would change if she could change one thing about her music class, she instantly replied, "I love singing and I just wish we could do more … I wish we had more time." I was surprised to hear that Destiny, a student who was often disciplined in music class and who frequently lost basketball and dance privileges because of her behavior in music class, had the same suggestion.

EMILY: How much singing would you do?
DESTINY: More. A lot of people don't like the singing in here [pause].
EMILY: Do you think singing is important?
DESTINY: Sometimes. It depends who's singing with them.
EMILY: Do you do much singing in this music class?
DESTINY: No.

A meaningful classroom, for Destiny, would include singing. However, the nature of the singing was important. Similarly, Tamila and Kesha described the ways in which singing can be meaningful in a music classroom. They emphasized variety and diversity. Tamila said, "We'll do all kinds to get all of them, so everyone could get a chance." Kesha had similar suggestions:

> I would aks them what do they want to sing about or what Ms. Miller
> does, basically, because Ms. Miller is the most fun music teacher I've
> had so far. I think the best singing class, I think you would have to
> switch it up sometimes. Sometimes do like some fun activities that have
> to do with singing and other things too. And then sometimes just stay
> laid back and just do the regular singing stuff that regular teachers do.

In my discussions with students about a hypothetical music classroom in which
they were the teacher, I was impressed with their comments about the specificities of singing in the music classroom. Surprisingly, many students emphasized singing range as something that was important to them. Both Precious
and Lori emphasized range when I asked them how they would teach. Precious
said, "Just well, just like, don't do songs that you know, go super high, and you
pushing to do it more and over and over again. Do songs … that's fun and
don't stress them out." Lori said she would have "more singing … More of
like, music that's low and fast." Tamila described the singing she would
incorporate into her music class. As mentioned earlier, she said, "My song
would be really long. A long note, but … truthful." When I asked her what
kind of music she would use to show "truthful," she replied, "I'd be really be
low. Or, kind of be like balancing high, have some highs and some lows in it."

The students imagined a classroom in which every voice was heard and
recognized, and each student's musical style was equally present within a collective whole. Their conception of a meaningful music classroom was a musically plural one. Many students emphasized the importance of student agency
within a culturally plural music classroom where student agency was achieved
when the teacher relinquished some of her power. An important form of
agency that students described was the freedom to be creative and imaginative.
They valued the opportunity to be creatively expressive, imaginative in composition, explore the instruments, or collaborate with friends. In addition to
being musically plural, the students' hypothetical music classroom would be
*vocally* plural, as well. Many of the students suggested that they would have
more singing in their classroom but that the type of singing was important.
They valued the use of diverse singing styles and experiences in the music
classroom and emphasized that this would allow all voices to be heard.

In their discussions about a hypothetical, meaningful music classroom, the
students shed light on whether their current music experience with the traditional music teacher or the non-traditional music teacher was in fact
meaningful. The students in the non-traditional music classroom in which
the teacher enacted culturally sustaining pedagogy used that classroom as an
example of a meaningful music experience. The students in the traditional
music classroom emphasized plurality and student agency as well as creativity in their hypothetical music classroom. Their conceptions of a meaningful music classroom were in stark contrast to what they experienced in
the traditional music classroom where they had little agency or opportunity
to uniquely express themselves.

Part IV

# Culturally Sustaining Pedagogy in Music Education

# 10 Musical Epistemology and Music Education

The overarching theme of this study is how the music classroom can be a site of liberation and individual empowerment. Conversely, educational sites can remain places where the hegemonic "norms, logic, values, and way of knowing" continue to enervate the spirit and potential of our students (Domínguez, 2017, p. 233). Based on Paris' (2012) conception of *culturally sustaining pedagogy*, I sought to expand upon previous research in culturally relevant and responsive music education (Fitzpatrick, 2012; Lind & McKoy, 2016; Shaw, 2014) as a means to discover the nuances beyond curriculum and repertoire that contribute to the continued cycle of exclusion within the field of music education. By looking specifically at the ways beliefs about the singing body were communicated to students in the general music classroom, I discovered that a Eurocentric musical epistemology invisibly inhabits all aspects of the classroom. Although cultural relevance has been explored in musical repertoire and curriculum, the nuances of pedagogy, classroom discipline, and beliefs about music and singing as they relate to race and world view in the music classroom remain to be fully dismantled.

Scholars, who have explored issues of race and racism within the field of music education (Bradley, 2015; Gustafson, 2009; Hess, 2015; Koza, 2008), agree upon the need to "call out" and "name" the injustices that continue to take place in music classrooms. Drawing from their work and that of scholars from the fields of education, educational policy, urban education, Afrocentrism, and Indigenous studies (Asante, 2011; Calderon, 2014; Domínguez, 2017; Gay, 2011; Mbembe, 2016; Milner & Tenore, 2010; Paraskeva, 2017; Patel, 2016; Quantz, 2011), this discussion situates my qualitative case study within discourses of coloniality, racism, epistemology, ritual, and pedagogical nuance. The goal is to uncover the ideology that allows for perpetuated racism in the field of music education.

## A Closed Musical Epistemology

### Coloniality

The discourse, approach, and method Ms. Greene employed in her music classroom are largely representative of the current approach in music teacher

DOI: 10.4324/9781003099475-14

## 108  *CSP in Music Education*

education and K-12 music classrooms in the United States. Although the interests of her students were different from those at previous institutions at which she had taught, Ms. Greene remained committed to the same music education discourses. These discourses specify methods, standards, pedagogy, singing, posture, repertoire, and classroom management that are grounded on a Eurocentric musical epistemology and deeply situated in a White, colonist world view (Gustafson, 2009; Hess, 2015). Although Ms. Greene certainly was not purposefully enacting a White supremacist ideology in her classroom, the normative music education practices to which she attended allowed for the perpetuation of this ideology and the simultaneous silencing of her students.

The examination of racist, normalized ideology within American education is not new. Theoretical and practical conceptions of social justice in education have examined educational inequality (Gay, 2002; Ladson-Billings, 1995). More often than not, these attempts have reinstated the status quo because they were framed within the same Eurocentric paradigm. More specifically, "we continue to promote systems that claim justice and equity but remain firmly rooted in a framework of coloniality" (Domínguez, 2017, p. 229). *Coloniality*, according to Maldonado-Torres (2007),

> survives colonialism. It is maintained alive in books, in the criteria for academic performance, in cultural patterns, in common sense, in the self-image of peoples, in aspirations of self, and so many other aspects of our modern experience. In a way, as modern subjects we breathe coloniality all the time and every day.
>
> (Maldonado-Torres, 2007, p. 243)

Many of the normalized values found in music education are tied to a colonial history. These values are based on the belief that Western classical musical practices can transcend cultural differences. The assumption that Western classical music is universally appropriate is rooted in colonialist discourses of the "cultured" and "uncultured" and "high" and "low" art. These discourses of "superiority" emphasize what is appropriate and therefore worthy of being included in the music classroom. The students in Ms. Greene's class had accepted that their musical epistemologies were "inappropriate" for the music classroom. This was evident based upon how they described their music as "different" from the music in music class.

The students used the word "different" to describe the ways in which movement was absent from their music classroom experience compared with their home musical experience. Precious compared her home music with that of the music classroom: "I mean, it'll kind of be different from the songs from like the normal songs we sing [in music class], 'cause it kind of like, it kind of has a beat a little bit." Mercy emphasized that the singing in the classroom was "pretty different to the singing at home. The music at home is more upbeat and it's easier to dance to. The one in Miss Greene's, it's more just to listen to. You can't really dance to it."

The implicit message the students internalized was that their musical epistemologies were inappropriate for this particular music setting. Gustafson (2009) attempts to unravel the hegemonic justification of racist discourses of appropriateness and superiority. She provides an historical analysis of racist music education practices that continue to shape contemporary discourses, or what she describes as the "racial incitements that underpin how one is supposed to think about music, learn it, listen to it, and perform it" (p. 201). She argues that "although these are presented as pedagogically *necessary* to participation, they are merely prescriptive of what has been heard and seen as racially specific to fabricated qualities of whiteness" (p. 201). Gustafson's analysis was largely prompted by her recognition of the high attrition rate of African American students in music programs and her observations of the ways African American children were alienated in elementary music classrooms. To uncover the deeply entrenched belief system from which today's music education practices stem, she "reject[ed] the idea that schools and teachers were the root of the problem" and instead "focused on comparisons of motion, speech, and singing that made one child's entrainment superior to another's" (p. 200). From this standpoint, Gustafson revealed a network of debilitating practices.

Gustafson's (2009) emphasis on the historical, social, and aesthetic "web" of ideology underpinning music education practices is comparable to Patel's (2016) call for a decolonization of educational policies and analyses that perpetuate racism within the field of educational policy. Much like Gustafson, she is interested in a radical unveiling and dismantling of systemic oppression by countering the ways in which imperialist discourses protect whiteness. One example she provides is the way in which dominant discourses allow for the segmentation of larger oppressive systems, and, in doing so, trivialize or deemphasize the harm suffered (p. 123).

Gustafson (2009) and Patel (2016) address the complexity of educational inequality by attending to sociocultural, historical, contemporary, and epistemic factors. Gustafson asserts that "abandoning the historic role played by race in music would duplicate denial of its alliance with notions of whiteness" (p. 124). It is with this same reasoning that I frame the discussion about culturally sustaining music pedagogy. To discuss how music is taught in K-12 schools in the United States within a framework of culturally relevant pedagogy without recognizing the broader, historical, philosophical, and epistemological influences allows for the perpetuation of neo-colonialist discourses about music and culture. It was because of the ways in which this framework has limited discussions of cultural equity in the music classroom that I sought a broader means by which to analyze how discourses about culture manifest in the music classroom.

### Method without Reflection

For Ms. Greene, her Orff training provided a sense of security and systemization that she did not receive in her college training. Her pedagogical approach remained uniform in all the educational settings in which she

## 110   CSP in Music Education

taught. Despite recognizing that her current students have "different interests" she assumed the universality of her methods rather than considering the context in which she was teaching, thus prioritizing her method over the interests of her students. For Allsup and Westerlund (2012), this is indicative of "an ethical crisis ... in music teacher preparation and music education methodologies when in the process of securing ends against the uncertainties of change, creative or imaginative options are foreclosed or limited" (p. 127). In addition, Allsup and Westerlund emphasize that "a fixed methodological view secures that the teacher need not reflect between choices" (p. 136). Prescriptive methods allow teachers to maintain universal and "color blind" assumptions about music, culture, and what is best for their students. Because these methods require little attention to students' interests, musical world views, and cultures, teachers are able to "perform" as teachers with little more than a superficial engagement with their students. The lack of engagement between teacher and student allows for an "ontological distance" (Domínguez, 2017, p. 228) and alienation in the music classroom.

In his discussion about decolonial teacher education, Domínguez (2017) asserts that the ontological distance between teachers and students of color contributes to the perpetuation of coloniality in education:

> In education, ontological distance refers to the vast, affective terrain ... between the practices, knowledges, and goals that are recognized in schools and beyond as valid and normative ... and an evolving multitude of others ... present and vivid in the lives of youth of color ... that at least at present, continue to be denied institutional validity.
>
> (Domínguez, 2017, p. 228)

Others in the field of music education have recognized the ways in which prescriptive music methods contribute to a distancing between student and teacher and to alienation in the classroom (Benedict, 2009; Hess, 2015). Students are alienated from teachers and teachers

> who presume to own the mode of production, are in reality alienated from the educative process as they are, in reality, handmaidens to a discourse of normative and commonsense social production of what counts as knowledge and unfortunately, in many cases, what counts as music.
>
> (Benedict, 2009, p. 219)

Therefore, although Ms. Greene used her methods to control what she believed to be uncontrollable students, in doing so she in fact was abdicating her own agency as a teacher and musician. In addition, Benedict (2009) posits that "the implementation of these methods in a strict and unmindful manner, often alienates both teacher and student from musicking" (p. 217). A systematic implementation of traditional music teaching methods, rooted in a Eurocentric musical epistemology, created distance between Ms. Greene and her students and alienated them from meaningful music-making.

Ms. Greene's use of pre-programmed curriculum and lesson plans absolved her from acquainting herself with her students and their musical interests. The distance between Ms. Greene's assumptions about her students and their lived realities quickly became apparent in my interviews. One example was Ms. Greene's assertion that her students did not want to sing. Subsequent interviews with students revealed that they in fact wanted *more* singing in the classroom. The lack of understanding and communication between Ms. Greene and her students was apparent but very little was done to close the distance and better understand the students' perspectives.

The harm created by an ontological distance between teacher and student is that it allows the teacher to "other" the student—to ignore the student's humanity. Most importantly, ontological distance relieves teachers from empathic engagement with their students. In the following section, I will expound upon the ways in which the ontological distance, created by the systematic use of Eurocentric methods, manifested in Ms. Greene's classroom as an objective racialization and disciplining of bodies.

### Racialized Bodies and Voices

Embedded within traditional American music teaching curriculum are Western classical aesthetics and values which delineate acceptable ways of receiving and making music. While these aesthetics and values certainly provide meaning for many, the unquestioned veneration of these values at the expense of other music epistemologies is problematic. In the area of vocal pedagogy, the traditional emphasis on "pure" head voice and the quiet listener, both in body and in voice, allows for the racialization and marginalization of diverse students in music classrooms. Historically, colonialist beliefs about vocal and musical inferiority, tied to a European bourgeois world view, justified the use of vocal teaching to discipline and control the colonized (Olwage, 2004). Much of the colonialist discourse was rooted in an antagonism between the "civilized" and the "savage other." Remnants of these discourses are woven into the fabric of contemporary music practices but unrecognizable as such. However, because of these normalized discourses, children continue to be excluded from music classrooms. This exclusion oftentimes occurs on the epistemological level. When children's musical epistemology—"the norms, logic, values, and way of knowing" music—conflicts with the normalized musical epistemology in classrooms and teacher education programs, they are often silenced (Domínguez, 2017, p. 233). One example of the ways in which children's musical epistemologies are silenced in the music classroom relates to the racialization of entrainment—"the way we react to music, with reference to the interaction of sound, memory, body, motions, and gestures" (Gustafson, 2009, p. xii).

## 112 *CSP in Music Education*

Within a Eurocentric musical epistemology, the experience of listening to music is one in which the mind and body are separated, whereas within African American and many non-Eurocentric traditions, music listening cannot be divorced from the body. Ms. Greene's training in a Eurocentric musical epistemology meant that while listening to music or singing, she expected students to have "hands down, touch your legs ... singing posture, sitting on pockets, legs are down flat, back is nice and straight and tall." Notes like these about body stillness and containment are consistent throughout my field notes. There was little or no opportunity for children to experience music with their bodies. Although Ms. Greene emphasized the values of movement within the Orff method, movement within this paradigm is defined as clapping, snapping, or slapping one's legs. Orff body percussion, ironically, is one in which the student is in fact separated from his body. Rather than allowing students' listening experiences to be an opportunity for personal entrainment, students are prescribed body percussion patterns or mandated to sit quietly and listen. Regardless of the students' ethnic backgrounds, the music classroom is therefore racialized, where Eurocentric values of music listening are normalized. Students are denied the opportunity to experience music in ways that may be more epistemologically congruent or, worse, they are punished when they experience music in ways unfamiliar to a Eurocentric musical epistemology.

In my interviews, it became apparent to me that the singing voice, for these students, could not be separated from the body. The conception of the "singing body" carried important epistemological meaning for the students' vocal identities. Singing which took place in the music classroom that involved still bodies and good posture was antithetical to their conceptions of singing. For many of them, the music and singing in the music classroom took place with a still body, whereas the music and singing at home was expressed with the moving body. In the music classroom, Gustafson notes that "the good ear is recognizable as the listener who paid attention to rhythmic detail but made no indication of it" (Gustafson, 2009, p. 153). The students' delineation between music embodiment (or lack thereof) inside the classroom and out indicated that they internalized this normative discourse about musical entrainment. Their musical epistemologies—the ways they knew, embodied, and experienced music—were not "appropriate" for the music classroom. The "appropriate" way to experience music in the music classroom was one in which the body and mind were separated.

### The Singing Body

Music curriculum and pedagogy based on a Eurocentric musical epistemology partitions music learning into the elements of music—harmony, melody, rhythm, among others—which can be separately studied. Western classical vocal pedagogy similarly identifies separate categories, such as posture, breath, and onset, with which to understand the *bel canto* singing technique.

*Music Epistemology and Music Education* 113

This approach to teaching, although seemingly unproblematic within a Eurocentric epistemology, assumes that the parts can be separated from the whole. Within a Eurocentric paradigm, one experiences music cognitively without body movement. Within a Eurocentric paradigm, one sings without the need for overt body gesturing. These undisputed ways of singing and experiencing music are in direct opposition to non-Western musical epistemologies. According to Merriam and Kim (2008, p. 76):

> If there's anything that non-Western systems of learning and knowing have in common, it's the notion that learning involves not only the mind but the body, the spirit, and the emotions. There is no separation of the mind from the rest of our being.

The students' perceptions of singing and the music-learning in Ms. Greene's classroom illuminated the ways in which a Eurocentric musical epistemology was hindering *my* understanding of their experiences. I realized I was framing the notion of a "silenced singer" within a Eurocentric framework where the singing voice is divorced from the singing body. For these students, however, to be a silenced singer was to in fact have the singing *body* be silenced. The singing body and singing voice were inseparable.

Gustafson (2009) sheds light on the ways in which discourses about body entrainment and head tone have manifested in the elementary music classroom. Historically, she notes that operatic singing stressed the subdued demeanor of the body's upper half. At the other end of the continuum, slave songs included pitch variance, extroverted body accentuation, and gestures viewed as foreign compared with the *bel canto* art that was embraced as native to American singing (p. 128).

Historically, musical embodiment was in direct opposition to the "subdued" aesthetics of *bel canto* singing. The use of "head voice" in elementary music teacher education and the "concentration on the upper body" allows for the "discouragement of rhythmic gesturing or bodily accentuation of any kind" (Gustafson, 2009, p. 129). Robinson-Martin (2010, p. 45) notes that in

> Singing genres outside of classical art music ... the vocal quality most often used is the ... belt quality [which] is not only different from vocal qualities found in classical in terms of timbre but is also different in terms of its physical production.

While Robinson-Martin (2010, 2017) focuses on the anatomical physicality (embodiment) of a belt vocal sound, Gustafson (2009), from a socio-historic perspective, shows how the physical embodiment of belting—found in non-*bel canto* singing styles—is juxtaposed with the aesthetics of head tone dominant singing: "The definition of belting for some is vocal production that comes from below the neck. The 'cultured' style of singing emphasizes restraint and polish that downplays the chest and vocal folds" (Gustafson,

## 114   CSP in Music Education

2009, p. 129). Although the use of the head voice in itself is unproblematic, it is the entanglement of the racialized historical ideology—"refined white voice versus harsh black voice"—with normalized pedagogical approaches—pure head tone, still body—that allows for the continued alienation of students in music classrooms.

Throughout my observations and student interviews, I came to realize that the singing culture emphasized in Ms. Greene's class and normalized in music teacher education was in direct opposition to many of these students' musical epistemologies. Robinson-Martin (2010) emphasizes the "vocal sounds and colors most commonly found in music outside of the classical art music ... [are] more closely related to that of vernacular or colloquial speech" (p. 45). The emphasis on speech, both in articulation and range, requires more of a chest-heavy or mixed vocal register.

The use of head voice and "proper" singing posture are inextricably linked. "Proper" singing posture consists of a still body and was described by students as being "strict." This was in opposition to students' descriptions of their own singing, which was inseparable from movement. This embodiment of singing—or the singing body—is antithetical to the passive posture and isolated singing voice in the music classroom. Robinson-Martin (2017) describes the Black musical tradition as a "complete intertwining of black music and dance" (p. 4). For the students with whom I spoke from African and African American cultural backgrounds, the singing experience in the music classroom was foreign to their conception of singing. Because of the disconnect between the ways they experienced singing and home and at school, I discovered that students who had vibrant singing lives outside of school and for whom singing was important, were "inhibited singers" in the music classroom. Many described a shyness they only felt in the music classroom. The separation of singing from movement in the music classroom seemed to contribute to students' hesitancy and inhibition.

As I re-examined the findings from the students' interviews, I was confronted with this notion of "unvoiced speech" (Quantz, 2011). The students had clearly expressed a disconnect between Ms. Greene's teaching and the ways in which they experienced music outside of school. I was troubled with the notion that many of them felt inhibited from singing in the music classroom despite feeling confident to sing in their daily lives. In his critique of rituals—"those nonrational areas that we rarely think about or plan" (Quantz, 2011, p. 8) in school settings (which I have called "nuances")—to uncover "the ritual patterns that might be found in classrooms that work to reproduce privilege and the status quo" (p. 15), Quantz (2011) discusses "unvoiced speech" (p. 64). He suggests that "one must compare outward speech to inward speech and look for the contradictions of the moment ... [to] help lay bare the hegemonic workings of the dominant ideologies" (p. 64).

The students were able to articulate the ways in which the music teaching was "different" from what they knew. However, despite their dislike of the music experience, they had accepted that this was the way one experienced

## Music Epistemology and Music Education  115

music in school. School music values, rooted in colonialism and European bourgeois ideals, delineate the "appropriate" way to listen to music, experience music, and make music. Although these values clashed with the students' own musical "ways of knowing," they had accepted them as the dominant discourse. Gustafson (2009) observed the "injury to the embodied musical experience most meaningful to many children" (p. 196) that took place because of this dominant discourse. The "unvoiced speech" of Ms. Greene's students that could "help lay bare the hegemonic workings of the dominant ideologies" was in their nonverbal embodiment of inhibition, reluctance, dislike, and resistance to participating in the music classroom. Their acceptance of the dominant musical epistemology allowed for their own musical epistemologies to be silenced.

Gustafson (2009) states that "he or she finds it very onerous to become intimate with that which is antithetical to his or her core" (p. 196). For many of Ms. Greene's students, the musical epistemology in the classroom was "antithetical to [their] core" and caused them to feel alienated. Some students, like Alma, Isabella, Mercy, and Tamila responded to this alienation by retreating, thus feeling inhibited in their musical expression. Others responded to the alienation by reacting and thus subjecting themselves to discipline. A uniform approach to musical methods and pedagogy, all based on a Eurocentric musical epistemology, alienates students. Gustafson (2009) observed similar music classrooms "that delivered a rejection of the child's disposition" (p. 196) and she suggests that "the defense of culture by withdrawal is a reasonable response in the face of perceived threat" (p. 196).

For White educators, who are privileged by dominant discourses, the saliency of culture in minoritized children's lives is undetectable, particularly because the children's cultural epistemologies are not recognized within dominant epistemologies. The invisibility of minoritized students' cultural epistemologies within normalized education discourses does not, however, make them unimportant. Quite the opposite, it is their invisibility that makes their uncovering and recognition all the more pressing. As stated by Erickson (2010),

> Everything in education relates to culture—to its acquisition, its transmission, and its invention. Culture is in us and all around us, just as the air we breathe. In its scope and distribution, it is personal, familial, communal, institutional, societal, and global.
>
> (p. 35, as cited in Gay, 2018, p. 9)

By not recognizing students' epistemologies within our musical framework, we can never fully equitize music education. An understanding of epistemology reaches far beyond the confines of repertoire, method, and curriculum. An understanding of epistemology accounts for the nuanced interactions, and complex manifestations of culture in every aspect of a child's life. By understanding students' "ways of knowing" music, we can

## 116 *CSP in Music Education*

begin to uncover the unquestioned assumptions and normalized rituals within our music classrooms that perpetuate the cycle of exclusion and contribute to the disempowerment of students.

## Culturally Sustaining Pedagogy and an Open Musical Epistemology

### *Discourses of Appropriateness*

Musical exclusions are part of a larger practice of cultural and linguistic exclusions. In their discussion about language as agency and sustenance for marginalized youth, Bucholtz et al. (2017) contend that students' linguistic practices must be sustained in the classroom, including "realms of cultural practice that tend not to be recognized as such and are instead often pathologized as evidence of cultural, intellectual, or moral deficiency" (Bucholtz et al., 2017, p. 45). This discussion is especially salient for music educators. Does the emphasis on traditional and prescriptive music teaching methods, both in teacher education and in the K-12 classroom, pathologize musical practices that fall outside the realm of the Western classical canon? Is there room within our musical parameters for hip hop, Spanglish, belting, Arabic *mawaal*, and dancing?

Rosa and Flores (2017) explore the ways in which "discourses of appropriateness ... are complicit in normalizing the reproduction of the White gaze by marginalizing the linguistic practices of language-minoritized populations in U.S. society" (p. 186). They discuss how "discourses of appropriateness" are tied to notions of "high" and "low" language forms—much like discourses about "high" and "low" musical forms (classical or nonclassical). Language hierarchy allows for the justification of "academically appropriate," and in doing so, "inappropriate" language. Students are told that the linguistic practices that form the basis of their identities are not appropriate for the classroom. The repercussions of these discourses are that students feel alienated, inhibited, or silenced in the classroom. In what ways do musical discourses of "appropriateness" allow for the pathologization of students' musical practices? How might music educators harness rather than silence their students' rich and diverse musical cultures?

### *The Paradox of Classroom Management*

Discourses of "appropriateness" permeate all aspects of a classroom. Normalized beliefs about the ways in which students should *be* in a classroom are culturally specific and racialized. Teachers are encouraged to prioritize discipline and the management of their classroom. However, as Gay (2011) suggests, responsive teaching deems classroom discipline unnecessary. In my classroom observations, I found Gay's assertion to be true. The teacher who emphasized prescriptive methods struggled with student behavior and therefore spent most of her time focused on classroom management, whereas the teacher who engaged with students in ways that were culturally affirming, in music, singing, banter, and dialect, spent little time on classroom management.

Similarly, Monroe and Obidah (2004) found, in their case study, the ways in which cultural synchronization in the classroom made classroom management unnecessary. In their 36 classroom observations and interviews with an African American middle school teacher and her mostly African American students, they discovered that "the teacher and students' shared cultural orientation influenced the teacher's responses to behaviors traditionally defined as disruptive in research literature" (p. 258). Of significance was the teacher's use of playful banter and humor in the classroom and this was incorporated using dialect and "linguistic and colloquial student expressions" (p. 263). Although the teachers I observed did not have the same cultural background as their students, the teacher who chose to respond and communicate in ways that were culturally meaningful, Ms. Miller, did so because she had taken the time to get to know her students. She valued the musical, linguistic and cultural competencies of her students over prescriptive methods that delineate the "appropriate" way of experiencing and responding to music.

### Culture Sustains

Ms. Miller, who celebrated the musical competence of her students in her teaching, enacted *culturally sustaining pedagogy* in her classroom. In doing so, she embodied what Bucholtz et al. (2017) emphasize as the reason for culturally sustaining teaching—simply, that "culture sustains" (p. 45). Teachers who uplift students' cultural epistemologies empower their students. Ms. Miller's attention to the culturally nuanced ways in which her students experienced music, singing, and speech created an environment in which they could each find their voice and feel empowered to musically express who they were. The complexity and nuance of language, communication, and expression within a child's particular way of knowing music or "musical epistemology" make that specific musical epistemology unique. The extent to which these nuances or "rituals" (Quantz, 2011) are recognized or not within a music classroom determine the extent to which a child is empowered, distanced, or silenced.

> In other words, ritual is not merely a technique, a method for improving learning, it is an agonistic space of meaning-making that is worth struggling over—it is where the real work of schooling takes place and unless we are attuned to it, we will never be able to move toward the hope of a transformative education that many of us embrace.
>
> (Quantz, 2011, p. 18)

Quantz's (2011) discussion about rituals in educational settings provides a framework through which we can consider culturally sustaining music teaching as well as ways to attend to ritual in music education. In her

## 118 *CSP in Music Education*

teaching, Ms. Miller attended to rituals of humor, dialect, and singing style that were familiar for her students. She allowed for movement and dialogue outside of normalized discourses of silence and stillness. By attending to the nuances that were meaningful for her students, she provided a classroom culture which was safe and uplifting for all of her students to express themselves authentically. How might teacher education attend to the nuances, the non-rational interactions, the sometimes-enigmatic territory in which students and teachers alike make meaning? How might teacher education expand to include alternative musical epistemologies—laterally not hierarchically?

### Beyond a Eurocentric Framework

Scholars from multiple disciplines who have sought to expand the epistemic horizons of their field emphasize the need to first dismantle, deterritorialize, decolonize, and then engage in "epistemic travel" to envision new possibilities towards a liberation of both the teacher and student (Asante, 2011; Calderon, 2014; Domínguez, 2017; Gould, 2012; Mbembe, 2016; Paraskeva, 2017). Drawing from those studies, in the following sections I will discuss ways in which the field of music education might decentralize the Eurocentric musical epistemology and embrace Paraskeva's (2017) conception of an *Itinerant Curriculum Theory* towards epistemic diversity and equality.

In the fields of curriculum studies (Calderon, 2014) and educational policy (Patel, 2016), both Calderon and Patel emphasize the need to extend beyond Eurocentric epistemologies and structures to dismantle coloniality in education. Calderon states, "Unfortunately, critical discourses (e.g., critical race theory, queer theory, etc.) based in Western epistemologies fail to decolonize settler colonial ideologies and practices by centering modern nation-state such as racial remedies" (Calderon, 2014, p. 315). Patel (2016) suggests that "the maintained belief that a colonial society's structures can provide the infrastructure within which noncontingent emancipation can take place is, therefore, a colonizing theory of change" (p. 118). Similarly, attempts within the field of music education and the broader field of education to equitize curriculum and practice have been largely unsuccessful because they have remained within the same Eurocentric framework (Hess, 2015; Paris & Alim, 2017). Because of this framework, the saliency of epistemological nuances, such as body entrainment and vocality, were unrecognizable. A true dismantling requires an epistemological shift as well as a reckoning of the ways in which racist discourses are embedded in music education traditions.

The process of decolonization and the dismantling of hegemonic Eurocentric discourses require the "naming" of injustices (Bradley, 2015; Gustafson, 2009). The disciplining of students' bodies as they engage with music, both in listening and singing, silences their "singing bodies." Therefore, by "calling out" musical discourses that allow for the racialization of students' bodies and the silencing of body entrainment and vocal expression,

## Music Epistemology and Music Education   119

we can recognize the need for an expanded musical framework. Ms. Miller's teaching provided us with an opportunity to see what teaching beyond a Eurocentric musical epistemology might look like and the ways in which this teaching empowered rather than silenced students. By addressing the specific nuances within music teaching that continue to silence students, we can begin to "actively and intentionally disrupt and unsettle" (Domínguez, 2017, p. 233) the dominant music epistemology.

How might the field of music education disrupt and actively work to uncover coloniality in our practices? For scholars working to decolonize education, both in music and beyond, many emphasize the need for epistemic exploration—a cross-disciplinary, rhizomatic (Deleuze & Guattari, 1987) expansion of normalized practices—as a means of dismantling and re-envisioning educational practices (Asante, 2011; Calderon, 2014; Domínguez, 2017; Gould, 2012; Mbembe, 2016). Conceptions of rhizome within a music education framework allow for a cross-epistemic understanding of music in which the Western canon is decentralized and experienced only as it relates to a multitude of musical epistemologies.

### Epistemic Travel

The discussions I had with diverse fifth- and sixth-grade students prompted my own epistemic exploration; I found myself searching for something deeper, to examine the ways in which the field of music education could move beyond the bounds of a Eurocentric epistemology to embrace a hybridity of musical epistemologies. In this search I discovered Paraskeva's (2017) conception of an *Itinerant Curriculum Theory*. His radical approach to dismantling the canon and resurrecting marginalized epistemologies as a means of liberation, decolonization, and empowerment provided me with a framework.

To address coloniality in education, Paraskeva (2017) conceived of a theory that deterritorializes, decolonizes, and liberates by "calling out the Western Modern Eurocentric epistemicide" (p. 3). By addressing the "epistemicide"—the destruction of non-Eurocentric epistemologies—within educational practice and theory, we can begin to dismantle the ideological confines of coloniality in education. Paraskeva calls for educators to unveil the epistemologies erased by colonialism and dominant White discourses and expand beyond Eurocentric frameworks towards a rhizomatic coexistence of diverse epistemologies. Within the field of music education, much like Paraskeva, Gould (2012) emphasizes a rhizomatic, "transdisciplinary," and hybrid approach to dismantle musical elitism.

> Rhizomatic lines of flight connect the theoretical and political, include experiences from everyday life, conflate so-called high and low culture, and mix expressive modes .... Not only are ideas borrowed from one

120   *CSP in Music Education*

discipline to another, the hierarchies on which they are organized are deliberately subverted or deterritorialized.

(Gould, 2012, p. 82)

A rhizomatic and hybrid approach to music teaching disrupts the musical hierarchy, centers marginalized musical traditions in both heritage and emergent forms, and allows for a coexistence of diverse musical epistemologies. This approach to music teacher education provides teachers with the tools to recognize and attend to the cultural nuances of their students. In doing so, both teachers and students can be empowered.

In light of Domínguez's, Gould's, and Paraskeva's call for a rhizomatic, epistemic expansion, in what ways do contemporary music teaching practices a) perpetuate the erasure of non-dominant musical practices, b) deemphasize the contributions of marginalized musical communities, or c) repeat repertoire, lyrics, and jargon that are rooted in slavery and colonialism? How might the field of music education expand its epistemic horizons? In his discussion about "culturally sustaining and revitalizing pedagogies," Domínguez (2017) suggests that "epistemic travel" is vital to teacher education. Epistemic travel is the necessary step towards resurrecting agency in both teachers and students and closing the ontological distance between them. Discussions about musical cultures and curriculum are susceptible to becoming essentialized or fixed representations of culture; however, epistemic travel requires that teachers engage with a hybridity of musical epistemologies "in both heritage and emergent terms" (Domínguez, 2017, p. 233). By simultaneously "sustain[ing] and revitalize[ing] heritage practices and deeply rooted community wisdom, while nurturing the dynamic, evolving identities, ingenuity, and practices of historically marginalized and culturally diverse youth" (p. 225), teachers can empower their students. The notion of *epistemological* broadening is important because it allows for the musical practices, ways of knowing, and values in addition to musical content.

For the students with whom I spoke, singing and emotion, expression, embodiment, family, function, culture, and spirit were intertwined to form their musical selves. Their musical selves, composed of their musical and vocal identities, were comingled with other aspects of their identity, none of which could be separated from the whole. Music functioned as an integral and holistic part of their lives, inseparable from their families, emotions, and ways of being. Emotionally, many of the students described the ways in which music allowed them to express the complexities in their lives. Family and life experiences were interlinked with their musical expression as a cohesive whole. Their musical expression, experienced both physically and spiritually, was a whole-body encounter. This embodiment of music was relevant in all forms of musical engagement and learning, especially for singing. The singing voice encapsulated the singing body and singing spirit. In essence, their embodiment of music was an amalgamation of their whole selves, their families, and their life experiences.

The recognition of students' cultural practices in the classroom can be transformational for them. Therefore, as music teachers engage in epistemic exploration, they might ask themselves, "Are there practices that communities have sustained over time (albeit in hybrid forms and transformations) that have sustained communities to be resilient in the face of challenge?" (Lee, 2017, p. 266). Lee's question is particularly salient for music educators because music has played an important role in the struggle and sustenance of disenfranchised communities. I think of the ways in which the students I observed exuded joy, confidence, and passion when given the opportunity to musically engage in ways that were meaningful for them.

Culturally sustaining music teaching, teaching that is attentive of and responsive to students' musical epistemologies—their ways of knowing music—is less daunting than we might think. It is in the non-rational rituals, the nuances that occur in our music classrooms where Davion can freely call back to his teacher in affirmation of what she said without being reprimanded for not raising his hand; where Aisha, Luis, and Precious can freely embody the music without feeling inhibited; and where Isabella, Alma, and Mercy's vocal and linguistic competence is celebrated rather than silenced. Attending to music epistemologies allows teachers to more deeply and critically investigate the multifaceted ways in which students *know* music.

# References

Allsup, R. E., & Westerlund, H. (2012). Methods and situational ethics in music education. *Action, Criticism, & Theory for Music Education (MAYDAY Group)*, 11(1), 124–148.

Asante, M. (2011). *The afrocentric idea revised.* Temple University Press.

Benedict, C. (2009). Processes of alienation: Marx, Orff and Kodaly. *British Journal of Music Education*, 26(2), 213–224. doi:10.1017/s0265051709008444.

Bradley, D. (2015). Hidden in plain sight. In C. Benedict, P. Schmidt, G. Spruce, & Woodford, P. (2015). *The Oxford handbook of social justice in music education* (pp. 190–203). Oxford University Press. doi:10.1093/oxfordhb/9780199356157.013.14.

Bucholtz, M., Casillas, D. I., & Lee, J. S. (2017). Language and culture as sustenance. In D. Paris & H.S. Alim (Eds.), *Culturally sustaining pedagogies: Teaching and learning for justice in a changing world* (pp. 43–59). Teachers College Press.

Calderon, D. (2014). Uncovering settler grammars in curriculum. *Educational Studies*, 50(4), 313–338. doi:10.1080/00131946.2014.926904.

Deleuze, G., & Guattari, F. (1987). *A thousand plateaus: Capitalism and schizophrenia* (B. Massumi, Trans.). University of Minnesota Press.

Domínguez, M. (2017). "Se hace puentes al andar:" Decolonial teacher education as a needed bridge to culturally sustaining and revitalizing pedagogies. In D. Paris & H. S. Alim (Eds.), *Culturally sustaining pedagogies: Teaching and learning for justice in a changing world* (pp. 225–245). Teachers College Press.

Fitzpatrick, K. R. (2012). Cultural diversity and the formation of identity: Our role as music teachers. *Music Educators Journal*, 98(4), 53–59. doi:10.1177/0027432112442903.

## 122  CSP in Music Education

Gay, G. (2002). Preparing for culturally responsive teaching. *Journal of Teacher Education*, 53(2), 106–116. doi:10.1177/0022487102053002003.

Gay, G. (2011). Connections between classroom management and culturally responsive teaching. In C. M. Evertson & C. S. Weinstein (Eds.), *Handbook of classroom management: Research, practice, and contemporary issues* (pp. 343–370). Routledge. doi:10.4324/9780203874783.ch13.

Gay, G. (2018). *Culturally responsive teaching: Theory, research, and practice* (3rd ed.). Teachers College Press.

Gould, E. (2012). Uprooting music education pedagogies and curricula: Becoming-musician and the Deleuzian refrain. *Discourse: Studies in the Cultural Politics of Education*, 33(1), 75–86. doi:10.1080/01596306.2012.632168.

Gustafson, R. I. (2009). *Race and curriculum*. Palgrave MacMillan.

Hess, J. (2015). Decolonizing music education: Moving beyond tokenism. *International Journal of Music Education*, 33(3), 336–347. doi:10.1177/0255761415581283.

Koza, J. E. (2008). Listening for whiteness: Hearing racial politics in undergraduate school music. *Philosophy of Music Education Review*, 16(2), 145–155. doi:10.2979/pme.2008.16.2.145.

Ladson-Billings, G. (1995). Toward a theory of culturally relevant pedagogy. *American Educational Research Journal*, 32(3), 465–491. doi:10.3102/00028312032003465.

Lee, C. D. (2017). An ecological framework for enacting culturally sustaining pedagogy. In D. Paris & H. S. Alim (Eds.), *Culturally sustaining pedagogies: Teaching and learning for justice in a changing world* (pp. 261–273). Teachers College Press.

Lind, V. R., & McKoy, C. L. (2016). *Culturally responsive teaching in music education: From understanding to application*. Routledge. doi:10.4324/9781315747279.

Maldonado-Torres, N. (2007). On the coloniality of being: Contributions to the development of a concept. *Cultural Studies*, 21(2–3), 240–270. doi:10.1080/09502380601162548.

Mbembe, A. J. (2016). Decolonizing the university: New directions. *Arts and Humanities in Higher Education*, 15(1), 29–45. doi:10.1177/1474022215618513.

Merriam, S. B., & Kim, Y. S. (2008). Non-western perspectives on learning and knowing. *New Directions for Adult and Continuing Education* 119, 71–81. doi:10.1002/ace.307.

Milner IV, H. R., & Tenore, F. B. (2010). Classroom management in diverse classrooms. *Urban Education*, 45(5), 560–603. doi:10.1177/0042085910377290.

Monroe, C. R., & Obidah, J. E. (2004). The influence of cultural synchronization on a teacher's perceptions of disruption: A case study of an African American middle-school classroom. *Journal of Teacher Education*, 55(3), 256–268. doi:10.1177/0022487104263977.

Olwage, G. (2004). The class and colour of tone: An essay on the social history of vocal timbre. *Ethnomusicology Forum* 13(2), 203–226. doi:10.1080/1741191042000286167.

Paraskeva, J. M. (2017). Itinerant curriculum theory revisited on a non-theoricide towards the canonicide: Addressing the "curriculum involution." *Journal of the American Association for the Advancement of Curriculum Studies*, 12(1), 1–43.

Paris, D. (2012). Culturally sustaining pedagogy: A needed change in stance, terminology, and practice. *Educational Researcher*, 41(3), 93–97. doi:10.3102/0013189x12441244.

Paris, D., & Alim, H. S. (Eds.). (2017). *Culturally sustaining pedagogies: Teaching and learning for justice in a changing world*. Teachers College Press.

## Music Epistemology and Music Education 123

Patel, L. (2016). Reaching beyond democracy in educational policy analysis. *Educational Policy*, 30(1), 114–127. doi:10.1177/0895904815614915.

Quantz, R. (2011). *Rituals and student identity in education: Ritual critique for a new pedagogy*. Palgrave Macmillan. doi:10.1057/9780230117167.

Robinson-Martin, T. M. (2010). *Developing a pedagogy for gospel singing: Understanding the cultural aesthetics and performance components of a vocal performance in gospel music* (Doctoral dissertation). Retrieved from ProQuest LLC. (UMI No. 3424907).

Robinson-Martin, T. M. (2017). *So you want to sing gospel: A guide for performers*. Rowman & Littlefield.

Rosa, J., & Flores, N. (2017). Do you hear what I hear? Raciolinguistic ideologies and culturally sustaining pedagogies. In D. Paris & H. S. Alim (Eds.), *Culturally sustaining pedagogies: Teaching and learning for justice in a changing world* (pp. 175–190). Teachers College Press.

Shaw, J. T. (2014). *The music I was meant to sing: Adolescent choral students' perceptions of culturally responsive pedagogy* (Doctoral dissertation). Retrieved from ProQuest LLC. (UMI No. 3627141).

Part V

# Moving Forward Towards Culturally Sustaining Music Pedagogy

# 11 Practical Implications for the Music Classroom

To enact culturally sustaining pedagogy in music education, we must expand our epistemic boundaries and simultaneously deepen and widen our understanding of epistemologies of music. A necessary part of this process is recognizing our own world view and our assumptions about music teaching and learning that are framed within it. By shedding light on our beliefs, we can begin to interrogate and rethink that which we have come to believe is incontestable. The following practical exercises provide a means for music educators and teachers to question their own beliefs and practices.

## Critical Inquiry and Analysis of Current Practices

### *Music Teacher's Credo—What Are My Beliefs and Assumptions?*

Consider your beliefs about music teaching and learning—that which you have come to believe as universally applicable. Use the following guiding questions to devise statements about your beliefs.

### *Overarching*

- What are my normalized practices?
- What do I do every day in the music classroom?
- What do I believe as a music educator?
- What have I come to believe based upon my teacher education?

### *Discipline/Classroom Management*

- What do I believe is appropriate or inappropriate behavior in the music classroom?
- What are my rules?
- What behavior have I been taught to "correct"?
- What do I believe about student behavior?
- What are my assumptions about classroom discipline?

DOI: 10.4324/9781003099475-16

128   *Moving Forward*

*Vocality (Singing and Speaking)*

- What language have I been taught to "correct"?
- What singing styles have I been taught to "correct"?
- What are my beliefs about vocal technique?
- What type of vocality do I use?
- How do I engage my students with my singing and speaking voice?
- How do I speak to my students?
- Do my students sing freely in the classroom?
- Do they feel inhibited or nervous about singing?
- Do I allow them to sing in ways that are comfortable for them?
- Do I correct their singing?
- Do I correct their pitch?
- How do I approach vocal technique?
- Do I allow my students to belt while singing?
- Can I demonstrate belting?
- Do I allow my students to sing with a nasal tone, a dark and swallowed tone, or sing with vocalities not demonstrated by me?

*Movement*

- What body movements have I been taught to "correct"?
- What do I believe is appropriate musical embodiment in the music classroom?

*Methods*

- What do I believe about musical standards?
- What do I believe about music literacy?

*Listening*

- What do I believe is appropriate music listening behavior in the music classroom?
- How do we listen to music in the classroom?
- What types of music listening exercises do I do in the classroom?
- Do I require that my students listen quietly?

*Pathologized Forms of Music Engagement*

- What musical forms or ways of making music do I pathologize?
- What ways of experiencing music do I pathologize?

*Repertoire*

- What do I believe is appropriate repertoire for music teaching?

*Practical Implications* 129

- Am I aware of the histories of the music I employ in the general music classroom?
- Am I aware of songs with racist histories like "Camptown Races" and "Oh! Susanna"?

### Caring/ Knowing My Students

- What are my assumptions about my students and their musical backgrounds?
- How do I get to know my students?
- Do I know about my students' home lives?

### Interactions/Engaging My Students

- What type of body language do I use with my students?
- How do I engage my students?
- How do I interact with my students?

### Student Empowerment

- How do I empower and motivate my students?

### Music Teacher's Workshop—How Might I Interrogate That Which I Believe?

Now, consider the ways in which your beliefs impact your teaching and students. How do we come to believe what we believe? Use the following questions to guide your inquiry and interrogation of that which you had assumed to be irrefutable.

### Overarching

- What will happen if I allow musical sounds, musical movement, and musical behavior that I believe are incorrect or inappropriate to take place in the classroom?
- In what ways might my normalized practices be alienating?
- In what ways is my teaching impacted by my definitions of music success?
- Does my definition of music success prevent me from taking creative risks?
- In what ways do I allow the impressions of other teachers and staff to impact my creative agency as a teacher?
- Am I afraid to take risks? If so, why?
- Am I afraid to go beyond the bounds of Western classical music hierarchies of value and practice? If so, why?
- Do I employ methods without careful consideration of their impact?

130   *Moving Forward*

## Discipline/Classroom Management

- What will happen if I allow students the freedom to behave in ways that are more familiar for them?
- Are there certain prescribed rules to which I must adhere in order to feel like a successful teacher?

## Vocality (Singing and Speaking)

- Do I believe that I must achieve a unified vocal sound? If so, why?
- Do I pathologize and discourage certain ways of speaking and singing? If so, why?

## Movement

- Do I believe that all students must move in the same ways? If so, why?
- Do I discourage certain types of musical movement? If so, why?

## Methods

- Why do I value certain music teaching methods?
- In what ways do my teaching methods inform my beliefs about teaching and music-making?
- How do my students respond to my methods?
- Do I discourage certain musical activities and behaviors? If so, why?

## Repertoire

- Do I believe that certain repertoire is more appropriate than other repertoire? If so, why?

## Caring For/Knowing My Students

- Do I feel cautious about getting to know my students? If so, why?
- Is it hard for me to understand my students and their behavior?

### Music Teacher's Epistemic Expansion—How Might I Rethink My Practice and Assumptions?

With the following guiding questions, consider the ways in which you might expand your practice to incorporate a multi-epistemic approach to music teaching.

Practical Implications 131

## Overarching

- How might I re-think my beliefs about what is musically incorrect or correct?
- How might I incorporate an Afrocentric musical epistemology into my teaching?
- How might I incorporate an Indigenous musical epistemology into my teaching?
- How might I incorporate a Latinx musical epistemology into my teaching?
- How might I approach all aspects of my music teaching from multiple musical vantage points?
- How might I discover new ways of making music?
- How might I discover new ways of *knowing* music?
- How might I incorporate a wide range of musical epistemologies into my teaching?

## Discipline/Classroom Management

- How might I rethink the ways in which I consider discipline?
- How might I discover the underlying reasons of student disengagement rather than quickly punish or discipline?

## Vocality (Singing and Speaking)

- In what ways can our singing and speaking in the classroom recognize my students' vocal funds of knowledge—their vocal epistemologies?
- How might I re-think singing intonation to account for non-Western epistemological understandings of singing?
- How might I demonstrate various vocal timbres for my students and encourage them rather than discourage them?
- How might I empower my students with my speaking and singing?

## Movement

- In what ways can I allow my students to have freedom of movement and expression in the classroom?
- Can I allow the opportunity for free musical entrainment without pre-scribed movements, dance steps, or body percussion?
- Can I celebrate musical entrainment in the classroom as a means of empowering students' musical identities?

## Methods

- How do I find ways to implement my students' "funds of knowledge" into my teaching?

132    *Moving Forward*

- How might my teaching method reflect the cultures of my students rather than a method or curriculum to which I have prescribed?
- How might I broaden my understanding of the elements of music?
- How might I broaden my understanding of musical literacy?
- How might I demonstrate the value of oral musical traditions?
- How might I decenter musical literacy as a means to demonstrate the value of other musical ways of learning, transmitting and knowing?

### Listening

- How can I challenge Western classical assumptions about music listening?
- Can I allow my students to freely dance while listening? Make sound? Sing along?

### Repertoire

- How might my repertoire choices reflect the cultures of my students?
- In what ways can the repertoire I choose deepen my students' understanding of diverse musical epistemologies?

### Caring For/Knowing My Students

- How do I get to know my students?
- How do I care for my students?
- How do I create a safe space in which my students feel able to express themselves freely?

### Interactions/Engaging My Students

- How might I interact with my students in meaningful ways?
- How might I incorporate their ways of communication into my teaching?

### Student Empowerment

- How do I empower and motivate my students?
- How can I celebrate my students' musical-cultural identities in the classroom?

### Student Choice/Agency

- How do my students experience music outside of school?
- How would my students like to experience music in the classroom?
- How can I give students a choice and empower them in the classroom?

- In what ways can I allow my students to make curricular and musical choices in the classroom?

*Instruments*

- How might I allow my students to creatively explore instruments without prescribed rules and steps?

*Creativity*

- How might I incorporate more opportunities for my students to create and be creative agents of their own musical expression and entrainment?
- How might I incorporate musical creativity and composition in ways that differ from the way they are conceived within a Western classical epistemology?

## Case Study Exercise

The following exercise will apply the same reflective, analytical approach used in the previous exercise to a critical investigation of lesson plans and methods. For the next exercise, choose a music teaching lesson plan to analyze. Carefully consider the lesson plan from different vantage points. How might this lesson plan impact students from various backgrounds? The following is an example of the ways in which one might analyze music teaching lesson plans.

### Responding Units

The National Association for Music Education (NAfME), in partnership with the Library of Congress of the United States, developed music teaching curricula (Curriculum units, 2017–2020). The focus of the curricula is *Responding* to music and the NAfME standards with which this category is associated. NAfME divides this category into four sub-categories: select, analyze, interpret, and evaluate. The Responding units aim to teach students to:

- Select "music appropriate for a specific purpose or context" (Core music standards, 2014, p. 1).
- Analyze "how creators and performers manipulate the elements of music" (p. 1).
- Interpret "through their use of elements and structures of music, [how] creators and performers provide clues to their expressive intent" (p. 1).
- Evaluate "musical works and performances based on analysis, interpretation, and established criteria" (p. 1).

134    *Moving Forward*

While these aims at first glance may seem vague and perhaps unproblematic, upon closer inspection, their epistemological specificity becomes apparent. The first statement, under the category "select," assumes the universality of music appropriateness, thus presuming that for all people the same music would be used for the same specific contexts and purposes. Under the categories "analyze" and "interpret" it is assumed that all music includes a clearly delineated musical creator and performer and that the Western classical elements of music and musical structure are universally applicable. The fourth category, "evaluate," assumes that the listener can universally evaluate all music with pre-determined criteria. In addition, it is assumed that a pre-established definition of musical "quality" can be applied to the assessment of all music.

Similarly, the curricula overview demonstrates the epistemic specificity of the curricular approach. An emphasis is placed on music literacy because, as described in the overview, music literacy "reflect[s] the actual processes in which musicians engage" (Chorus responding unit, 2017, p. 4). In addition, the aim of the units is to "cultivate a student's ability to carry out the three Artistic Processes of Creating, Performing, and Responding," which they describe as "the processes that musicians have followed for generations" (p. 4). The curricula overview demonstrates the ways in which the curriculum, perhaps unbeknownst to the developers, is deeply steeped in normalized Western classical music assumptions. To equate music literacy with "the actual processes in which musicians engage" presumes that there is no other way for musicians to engage with music and denigrates those who engage with music differently. Similarly, the assumption that the linear, pre-supposed method of "Creating, Performing and Responding" is universally applicable excludes musical traditions that favor collectivist and holistic approaches, where music is not an individualistic undertaking, where musical engagement is not linear but cyclical, and the creation of music is not finite but ongoing.

The epistemological limitations of the curricula overview are also evident within the individual units. The following analysis of two units from this curriculum project will shed light on the ways in which assumptions that are normalized within a specific musical epistemology manifest in curriculum.

### Choral Pre-High School Unit

The first unit, a pre-high school choral unit on African American spirituals, demonstrates the ways in which the limitations of a Eurocentric musical epistemology fails to account for the epistemic specificities of this African American musical tradition. Over the course of four lessons, students are introduced to recordings and scores of three African American spirituals. The learning objectives that are outlined within each lesson focus on musical analysis and an evaluation and comparison of the recordings and scores. Students are asked to "analyze the performance in relation to the musical elements (pitch, rhythm, harmony, dynamics, timber, form, and style/

*Practical Implications*   135

articulation) contained in the score" and evaluate the performance based upon their analysis (Chorus responding unit, 2017, p. 16). Using the elements of music to evaluate and analyze, students are asked to identify how the "composer manipulated the musical elements" (p. 9) and are guided in their analysis with questions and activities. In addition, they are asked to "identify characteristics" they heard in recordings and "observed in the written notation" (p. 23). Then, they are asked to describe how the notated music facilitated their interpretation of "what the composer intended to express" (p. 24) and how the characteristics they heard in the music facilitated their interpretation of "what the performer intended to express" (p. 24). One activity simulated a music competition in which the student is asked to adjudicate and evaluate a recording of the African American spiritual "Good News" based upon the score, the elements of music that they recognize in the recording and score and their "understanding of this style/genre and choral music in general" (p.17).

NAfME's National Music Standards on which this curriculum unit is focused include: students' ability to "explain how the analysis of passages and understanding the way the elements of music are manipulated inform the response to music" (NafMe, 2014, p. 5); and students' ability to "explain and support interpretations of the expressive intent and meaning of musical works, citing as evidence the treatment of the elements of music, contexts, (when appropriate) the setting of the text, and personal research" (p. 5).

While the focus on African American spirituals is a positive deviation from curriculum solely based on Western classical music, the pedagogical approach of this unit remains rooted in a Western classical music epistemology (Chorus responding unit, 2017). For African American spirituals to be fully understood, however, this approach is inadequate. It is inadequate because it forces an Afrocentric musical tradition into a Eurocentric mold. By doing so, Western classical musical concepts that are irrelevant for Afrocentric music traditions are used in a haphazard manner to assess the music. Additionally, a Western classical epistemology is void of the language and musical conceptions inherent to African American spirituals. Therefore, a Western classical music epistemology limits this curriculum both because of its presumed musical universality as well as its effacement of non-Eurocentric musical epistemologies.

A Western classical musical epistemology prioritizes the composer, the score, and a musician's ability to read and accurately represent that which the composer notated. Within this paradigm the value of musical literacy is incontestable and the ability to analyze and deduce a musical score to the elements of music is an invaluable skill. Many non-Eurocentric music traditions, however, are not score and composer-centric. Particularly for music that is orally transmitted, like African American spirituals, the imposition of a musical score or transcription is contrived and limiting.

The scores used for this curricular unit (Chorus responding unit, 2017) were transcribed by White musicians. Many years ago, Seward, a Tonic Sol-Fa advocate and director of the Fisk Jubilee Singers, transcribed their songs

136  *Moving Forward*

to, as he described "[give] these melodies to the world in a tangible form," and "to say a few words about them as judged from a musical standpoint" (Marsh, 1880, p. 121).[1] Seward's assumption, rooted in a Eurocentric epistemology, was that his transcription and musical analysis of the songs would legitimize the music. Despite his codification of the music, both he and Natalie Curtis Burlin—a White privileged classical musician from New York whose transcriptions are compiled in the *Hampton Series Negro Folk-Songs*, also used for this unit (Patterson, 2010)—recognized the ways in which a transcribed score betrayed the essence of the music (Burlin 1918; Marsh, 1880). Burlin notes that the songs, which were "originally extemporaneous ... sprang into life as the expression of an emotion, of an experience, of a hope" (p. 4). Moreover, she describes how "the songs passed from singer to singer and from one locality to another" taking "on variants in words and melody" (p. 5).

This curriculum unit (Chorus responding unit, 2017) prioritizes Western classical conceptions of a composer and a score by asking students to "analyze the performance in relation to the musical elements (pitch, rhythm, harmony, dynamics, timber [sic], form, and style/articulation) contained in the score" (p. 16) and "identify how the "composer manipulated the musical elements" (p. 9). The emphasis on a score and composer is antithetical to the historical saliency of this musical tradition. The musical score erases the cyclicality and vitality of the music by making it finite. In fact, the prioritization of a score invisibilizes the history, function, and transmission of African American songs.

The essence of orally transmitted music is its sustainability—its limitless ability to encapsulate the life-stories of those for whom it has provided meaning while simultaneously remaining anchored to the past. It is an intergenerational, boundless expression of histories. In her discussion about the power of African American arts to remember the past while embracing the future, Love (2019) quotes Feelings, an African American artist, who with his art strives to sustain African creativity:

> My soul looks back in wonder at how African creativity has sustained us and how it sill flows—seeking, searching, for new ways to connect the ancient with the new, the young with the old, the unborn with the ancestors.
>
> (Love, 2019, p. 100)

To privilege one single composer and score, therefore, is to deny the collective voices of each song, to ignore the complex and interwoven musical histories and cultural memories.

The prioritization of the elements of music and musical literacy within this curriculum communicates to students that Western classical music elements are universally applicable and appropriate for all music traditions. In addition, the activities that call for students to assess and evaluate the music based upon Western classical musical aesthetics within a simulated music competition teaches students that they can evaluate and rank all musical traditions based upon preconceived criteria from a musically specific paradigm. The curriculum, therefore, reinstates a musical hierarchy where Western classical music is prioritized and universalized. Instead, to teach about African American music with an Afrocentric musical epistemology, sustains and revitalizes African American culture in the music classroom. It is important not just for African American students but for all students to recognize its value defined within its own epistemic bounds.

*Kindergarten General Music Unit*

The second analysis is of the kindergarten "General Music Responding Unit" in which images, recordings, and activities are used to teach kindergartners about *genre* (General music responding unit, 2020). In the first lesson, students begin by listening to a recording of "The Stars and Stripes Forever" while looking at a slide of two images. The first image is of a marching band and the second of a banjo player. Afterwards, students are asked to discuss the images and share what they "already know" about each image and what they "wonder about" (p. 15) each image. Following this discussion, students repeat the same activity. After the second listening, students are asked to discuss which picture best represents the music. The third time, students march and incorporate body percussion while listening to the music. The teacher then discusses *presto* and *largo* tempi and discusses the importance of the composer. Following this activity, students listen to "Liebestraum" and mirror the slow movements that the teacher demonstrates (p. 16). Afterwards they discuss the musical tempo and style which leads to the explanation of genre. Finally, the teacher discusses the role of a marching band conductor, demonstrates a basic conducting pattern and shows a baton to students. In addition, the teacher shows an image of John Philip Sousa and explains "that Sousa was one of the most famous conductors in American history and that he lived more than a hundred years ago" (p. 26).

Subsequent lessons explore classical piano music and jazz as two additional genres of music. Students are asked to apply their knowledge of dynamics and tempo to evaluate the other musical genres. In addition, they are prescribed an ostinato pattern to play with rhythm sticks and shown the notation of that ostinato. Finally, students are encouraged to move to the music by marching as if they are in a marching band or "air-playing an instrument that might be used" (General music responding unit, 2020, p. 29) for the selected performance. Jazz is introduced to the students with an image and recording of Gerry Mulligan and a video recording of the Dave Brubeck quartet followed by a discussion about saxophones, woodwind instruments, the term *quartet*, and improvisation. Students explore improvisation on the instruments after watching a video of Duke Ellington improvising.

138 *Moving Forward*

The goals for the unit are for students to be able to "move and play instruments appropriately to different music"; apply their knowledge of tempo and dynamics as a means "to understand new music"; "compare and contrast" music which with they are familiar to "new music"; describe "how the composer/performer used musical ideas to share a thought or feeling"; "notate or record" their "musical ideas"; and "identify differences between various genres of music" (General music responding unit, 2020, pp. 14, 27, 34, 38). Much like the choral unit, this unit is strongly centered on a Eurocentric musical epistemology. Value is placed on notation, the elements of music, the composer, and the conductor. Students are taught Western classical music terminology and asked to apply this and what they know about Western classical music to other genres, thus communicating to students that music can be universally understood and analyzed using Western classical musical concepts. Body movement is prescribed and includes body percussion, marching, instrument air-playing, or following the teacher's movements. The lessons and goals outlined communicate an "appropriate" way to move and an "appropriate" way to play instruments.

In addition, the materials chosen for this unit (General music responding unit, 2020) demonstrate the ways in which the curriculum is exclusive. Of the six photographs chosen to accompany the four lessons, all six images were of White men. They included: three images of marching bands, one image of a banjo player, one image of Gerry Mulligan, and one image of John Philip Sousa. Despite the banjo being an instrument that originated in Africa and was brought to the United States by African slaves, the image chosen to represent the banjo is of a middle-aged White man. Similarly, the image of a jazz musician that was chosen was of a middle-aged White man. Of the recordings chosen for these lessons, eight are of Western classical compositions, two are of Sousa's "The Stars and Stripes Forever" performed two separate years, one is of Gerry Mulligan, one is of the Dave Brubeck Quartet, and one is of Duke Ellington. Of these 13 recordings, only one is of an African American performer.

The choice of recordings and images is emblematic of the lessons themselves. Time is spent to learn about John Philip Sousa, yet the origins of jazz are not discussed. While jazz music is included as a means by which to learn about different genres, the manner in which it is included is problematic. Of the three jazz performers included, only one is African American. Despite the meticulous attention to vocabulary, procedures, and "I can" statements, it seems that little effort is made to connect the music to culture. Rather than be an opportunity to engender confidence in students for whom the African American jazz tradition is meaningful, the curriculum seems to actively avoid making a cultural and historical connection.

The one-dimensional nature of standards and the reduction of musical concepts and goals to short statements ensures an epistemically narrow approach to music teaching and learning. This approach is an inadequate means by which to teach about the complexity and beauty of music, musical culture, and the multifaceted ways in which music is experienced throughout the United States and the world.

## Note

1 See Part II in this book for more detail on the history of Tonic Sol-Fa and the Fisk Jubilee Singers.

## References

Burlin, N. C. (1918). *Hampton series Negro folk-songs*. G. Schirmer. doi:10.5479/sil.523222.39088007761604.

Chorus responding unit: Teaching with primary sources. (2017). *A curriculum project of the National Association for Music Education and the Library of Congress of the United States*. https://nafme.org/wp-content/uploads/2017/08/Chorus-Responding-Unit-Proficient-Level.pdf.

Core music standards. (2014). *National Association for Music Education*. https://nafme.org/wp-content/uploads/2014/06/Core-Music-Standards-EUs-EQs-Definitions.pdf.

Curriculum units for the 2014 music responding standards. (2017–2020). National Association for Music Education and the Library of Congress of the United States. https://nafme.org/my-classroom/nafme-tps-curriculum-units-2014-music-responding-standards

General music responding unit, kindergarten level: Teaching with primary sources. (2020). *A curriculum project of the National Association for Music Education and the Library of Congress of the United States*. https://nafme.org/wp-content/uploads/2019/06/General-Music-Responding-Unit-Kindergarten.pdf.

Love, B. L. (2019). *We want to do more than survive: Abolitionist teaching and the pursuit of educational freedom*. Beacon Press.

Marsh, J. B. T. (1880). *The story of the Jubilee Singers: With their songs*. Houghton Mifflin. doi:10.5479/sil.44947.39088001640945.

Music standards, ensemble. NafME. (2014). *National Association for Music Education*. https://nafme.org/wp-content/uploads/2014/11/2014-Music-Standards-Ensemble-Strand.pdf.

Patterson, M. (2010). *Natalie Curtis Burlin: A life in Native and African American music*. University of Nebraska Press. doi:10.2307/j.ctt1dfnrrq.7.

# 12 Towards a Framework for Culturally Sustaining Music Pedagogy

Using *culturally sustaining pedagogy* (Paris, 2012; Paris & Alim, 2017) as a framework, this chapter will present *culturally sustaining music pedagogy* as a new theoretical framework with which to approach music teaching and learning from an equitable, justice-seeking, culturally affirming vantage point. This framework calls for a threefold approach to equitizing music education spaces: 1) dismantling, 2) expanding, and 3) embracing. The first step is to dismantle harmful, normalized practices that because of their assumed universality are invisible to those who are privileged by them. For students whose cultures are not recognized within a Eurocentric epistemology, to be given the opportunity to fully participate in the music classroom, it is essential that these practices be uncovered and dismantled. Second, culturally sustaining music pedagogy calls for an expansion of current music education practices to embrace non-Eurocentric musical epistemologies. This expansion must reach beyond previous attempts which merely expanded repertoire and curriculum to account for students' musical worldviews. Lastly, culturally sustaining music pedagogy requires an embracing of non-Eurocentric epistemologies as valuable entities within their own frameworks rather than viewing them through a Eurocentric lens. This requires a re-defining of musical "standards" to recognize diverse musical epistemologies.

## Dismantling

On their website, The National Association for Music Education (NAfME) provides a database of lesson plans and music teaching resources for their members (My Music Class[TM]). Using different search criteria, teachers can discover curriculum aligned with NAfME's musical standards. A cursory search for general music teaching curriculum using the search term "proper" produces 129 documents. This demonstrates the ways in which archaic discourses of "proper" and "not proper" continue to permeate our music teaching pedagogies. Why is one vocal technique more proper than another? Why, in fact, is much of our pedagogy focused on the binary of proper or improper, right or wrong?

DOI: 10.4324/9781003099475-17

Culturally sustaining music pedagogy requires that we scrutinize our assumptions, our beliefs—that which we have come to presume is incontestable. The dismantling of the belief system on which music teaching and learning is based, however, provides little benefit for the current majority of music teachers and administrators. In fact, the discourses and normalized practices used within the field of music teaching and learning, many of which have remained intact for 200 years, have prevailed because of the ways in which they benefit and privilege the status quo.

It is the cycle of exclusion, where those who have benefited perpetuate the same systems with which they were taught, that makes the dismantling of exclusive practices so difficult.

Normalized music teaching practices and ideology protect our music institutions. For many, these practices and ideology also protect our musical egos and musical identities. To question this ideology would require that we redefine that which has defined us as musicians, educators, performers, and musical consumers. Discourses of class, culture, elitism, civility, literacy, and expertise fuel our belief system and enliven our traditions. To question this ideology is to question our own value as educators and performers, experts and technicians. It is much easier to agree that the system is exclusive and should be changed than to actually change it. Change, especially change that dismantles that which we have spent our lives studying, mastering, and teaching, may seem futile, more harmful than good, and the benefits of doing so ambiguous. Systemic change, therefore, is selfless, empathic, and takes effort and courage. We must creatively and compassionately enact systemic change that will allow our music classrooms to be spaces of empowerment for all students. It is in the abdication of our traditions and assumptions that we can move towards culturally sustaining music teaching.

What practices and assumptions are problematic? Which practices alienate students from meaningful participation in their music class? There are four types of assumptions that must be interrogated: 1) beliefs and practices that protect our traditions and egos; 2) beliefs and practices that we believe will benefit or "improve" our students; 3) beliefs and practices that are seemingly neutral and universal; 4) beliefs and practices that are invisible.

To interrogate and dismantle the practices that protect our traditions requires that we ask ourselves why those practices are important. In a general music class, why must the students' singing voices blend? Why must their vowels and timbre be uniform? Can we let children choose their own vocality, even if it is more nasal or a darker tone color than that to which we are accustomed? Why must our listening practices be "disciplined" both in body and in focus? Can we allow children to musically express themselves with their bodies, without prescribing the movements that are acceptable? What would happen if we abandoned the notion of classroom management? What if we broke the rules that have robbed us and our students of creative agency, musical embodiment, and expression? What if we truly had fun in

## 142 *Moving Forward*

our music classroom and gave up methods that, if we are being truly honest, are oftentimes culturally exclusive, musically boring, and based on traditions of containment, regulation, and discipline? Can we interrogate our beliefs about "healthy" singing and the ways in which we use these discourses for power and authority? Can we identify the ways in which vocal intonation and aurality are subjective and culturally specific, and yet, within our Eurocentric paradigm, we use intonation to subvert, silence, discipline, and "improve" our students' voices? What do we pathologize? Do we pathologize singing and speaking that sound different from what we know? Do we try to change that with which we are unfamiliar? Or can we embrace and even adopt that which is uncomfortable?

The teacher in the case study, outlined in Part III of this book, who enacted culturally sustaining pedagogy, adopted the speaking and singing traditions of her students. She adopted the communication styles of banter and movement, which provided meaning for her students. How can we move past our traditions, the safe boxes in which we are enclosed, to find meaning and ways of making music within a much broader and richer landscape? Are we clinging to traditions because we are fearful of the unknown? Are we fearful of re-imagining our identities in broader and richer terms? Who or what is holding us hostage to our traditions?

To interrogate our "saviorist" assumptions and the practices we believe will benefit our students, we must be willing to abdicate the superiority of the Western classical tradition. Certainly, it has meaning for many, myself included, but the imposition of a sole musical tradition that is steeped in a Eurocentric epistemology on those for whom this tradition is not relevant is perpetuating coloniality. We are not helping, improving or saving, refining, bettering or disciplining our students by vehemently advocating for this tradition. Rather, we are communicating elitism, a musical caste system (musical classicism), and silencing the musical identities of our students. Our students will continue to participate in the rich musical traditions of their communities and families. They will continue to find spiritual and emotional reprieve with the musical traditions that have sustained their communities for generations, in continually evolving ways, regardless of the music we teach in our music classrooms. However, rather than have our music classrooms continue to be places in which they must abandon their identities because we are determined to instill that which is meaningful for us, we can re-imagine our classrooms to be places in which their identities are affirmed and recognized. We must consider Love's (2019) poignant question, "What good is education if you must shed who you are?" (pp. 38–39).

Schools and educational spaces are not devoid of ideology, culture, and normalized beliefs. If we continue to ground our music teaching and learning only on a Eurocentric epistemology, we will continue to ignore the epistemologies of our students. Just as schools are never neutral spaces, our teaching methods and practices are never neutral or universal. Therefore, we must interrogate the practices that we believe are absent of ideology and therefore universally applicable. The Orff teaching method is based on the belief system that music is evolutionary and that *ostinati* and the pentatonic scale are universally applicable. Inherent within this ideology is the supposition that children will evolve musically and become more musically complex. The problem with this belief system is two-fold. First, musical characteristics, like repeated rhythmic patterns and the pentatonic scale, are in fact characteristic of deeply intricate and complex musical traditions throughout the world. Therefore, the presentation of these characteristics as basic, tribal, and a precursor to more "complex" and "advanced" music reinforces a musical hierarchy within our music classrooms. Second, the ways in which the Orff method presents these "universal" musical characteristics are clinical in manner, supposedly devoid of particular cultural associations. As a result, the method reinstates the Eurocentric separation of musical elements, thus reinstating a Eurocentric music epistemology.

The assumptions most difficult to dismantle are those that are so ingrained within our teaching frameworks and methods that they have become invisible. We believe that head voice singing is the most "correct" and "pure" singing register for elementary music students, otherwise, they will experience vocal harm or damage. Perhaps we have not considered that many singing traditions around the world are devoid of the head voice register, yet their traditions remain alive without a massive number of people succumbing to vocal damage. Perhaps we have not considered that by "outlawing" or discouraging singing that does not primarily make use of the head voice register, we are communicating to our students that their singing traditions are "unhealthy." African American gospel singing, *Mariachi* singing, Arabic *mawaal*, Congolese singing, Malaysian *Dondang Sayang*, Croatian *Bećarac*, and Vietnamese *Ca trù* singing are just a few examples of vocal traditions that rely on a chest-voice dominant vocal production for meaning. The list is endless.

When we uncover the assumptions that are harmful and yet unrecognizable to us, we can begin to peel away the layers of musical hegemony and musical superiority that undergird our music teaching practices. In doing so, we can make room for our students' musical epistemologies—musical ways of knowing, singing, dancing, expressing, celebrating, and experiencing their cultural histories while envisioning their cultural futures. Our music classrooms have the potential to be full of rich and complex musical experiences, but first we must dismantle and uncover that which has and continues to hold us back from this possibility.

## Expanding

At the heart of culturally sustaining music pedagogy is the re-thinking of that which we have presumed to be "good" and "bad." Hip hop and popular music, if they ever have a place in our music classrooms, were there because we wanted to use them to teach more "advanced" musical concepts.

## 144  *Moving Forward*

Culturally sustaining music pedagogy, however, requires that we expand our definitions of acceptable music, acceptable singing, acceptable instrument-playing, acceptable behaviour, and acceptable language, to name a few. As we expand the borders of our curriculum, pedagogy, and methods, we must consider the ways in which we have pathologized non-Eurocentric conceptions of speech, movement, behavior, musical performance, and musical reception. It is our "etiquettes" that are preventing us from expanding our definitions of that which is "good."

Might we allow or even encourage our audiences to interact during the performance rather than penalize, humiliate, and silence those who experience music in non-Eurocentric ways? How might we break the rules in our performances to defy the traditions that discipline and subvert our students and our audience? How might we reconceive our rules about musical interpretation to allow our students to breathe life into a score? Might we allow them to scoop in a classical art song, change the notes, the dynamics, the words to make it more meaningful and relevant for them? How might we rethink and expand our instrument playing techniques? Can we allow our orchestra and band members to sit anywhere they would like on stage? For classical musicians and educators, some of these questions seem ludicrous and maybe even sacrilegious. However, teachers who are privileged by whiteness are unaware of the ways in which Black and Brown children have long suffered invisibility within schools and classrooms.

The United States Supreme Court decision that marked the beginning of this suffering and the desegregation of schools was *Brown v. Board of Education* (1954). Love (2019) equates school integration to colonization (p. 50). She, Derrick Bell (Trei, 2004), and others (Fairclough, 2004; Morris, 2008) interrogate the dominant narrative of school integration as educational saviorism. In fact, Morris (2008), in his counternarrative, illuminates the presumptive misconceptions that led to the Supreme Court decision. Undergirding the decision was a disregard for the "value of African American culture and institutions in the sustenance of Black people" coupled with the assumption "that White culture had much to offer Black people ... [but] the reverse did not hold true" (p. 717).

The dominant narrative, then and now, was that school integration would provide better schooling for African Americans. Absent from this narrative are the ways in which school integration stripped African American children of their cultural communities. Education for African American children, prior to *Brown v. Board of Education* (1954), was a collective community effort. African American children were taught by African American teachers who taught in ways that were culturally sustaining, culturally affirming, and drew on the cultural wealth of their community. Children were taught in ways that were familiar and therefore clearly understood what was expected of them. These expectations were not just curricular but also extended to communication style and classroom behavior. Children were taught by teachers who cared about their success and cared about them. Morris' (2008) counternarrative depicts the ways in which parents and community members were deeply conflicted about school integration. Integration would, ostensibly, provide more and better resources for African American students; however, this was at the expense of culturally sustaining teaching. The risk, described by Morris, was "for Black children and their culture to be totally ignored in the curriculum and the culture of the school" (p. 718).

Counternarratives require that we question our assumptions. They require that we expand our epistemic understanding of that which we have come to believe is true. The importance of shedding light on this counternarrative is twofold. White Americans' saviorist attempts to use schooling to "improve" and "assimilate" African Americans, Native Americans, and those for whom White dominant culture was not familiar, in fact did the opposite. Mainstream Eurocentric schooling robbed students of their cultural ways of knowing and culturally sustaining education—informally within the community or formally within schools. For the African American parents, community members, and teachers who were concerned that school integration would erase their children's culture from their schooling, their fears came to fruition. In addition, the counternarrative demonstrates the efficacy and intentionality of African American schools prior to integration and the ways in which they valued culturally sustaining education. This demonstrates that the cultural deprivation model on which *Brown v. Board of Education* (1954) was based was unsubstantiated. By recognizing the harm that school integration did to African American schools and the cultural harm that continues to take place in Eurocentric schools, this counternarrative forces us to contemplate the ways in which our educational system and we are accountable.

Almost 70 years after *Brown v. Board of Education* (1954), children's cultures are still absent from their schooling. Their cultural ways of knowing and being are not recognized in curriculum, classroom management strategies, pedagogy, and school culture. It is, therefore, consequential that teachers for whom a Eurocentric epistemology is comfortable widen their vantage point and expand their understanding to better empathize with all of their students. Counternarratives challenge teachers to expand their epistemic understanding of the ways in which schooling and teaching practices impact students. By doing so, we prioritize our students' humanity over archaic traditions. Through expansion, we can re-imagine the boundaries of our teaching practice and in doing so, truly affirm our students.

## Embracing

The expansion of our music teaching practices is not possible without an epistemic expansion of our musical frameworks towards a multi-epistemic and multi-centric approach. Our teaching must be Afrocentric, Indigenous-centric, Latinx-centric, in addition to Eurocentric. We must simultaneously

## 146 *Moving Forward*

offer access to Western classical notation, aural transmission, and musical story-telling as means by which to transmit musical culture. We can teach the "elements" of music as one approach within one musical epistemology. We must also, though, teach holistic music, music ecology, music and spirit, and music and place. Instruments can be played in a multitude of ways. Singing voices can embrace a multitude of timbres and vocal sounds. Intonation can be presented in a Western classical way or in an Afrocentric way where emotion and feeling guide the pitch (Robinson-Martin, 2017). Music listening can be active both physically and vocally or passive with a staid body. We must not limit ourselves as we redefine musical literacy, musical standards, musical expressivity, music appreciation, and musical performance while adding new terms that allow for an expansion of our musical world views.

We must empower our students to push the boundaries rather than be beholden to methods and techniques. In his analysis of the history and influence of African American music, Wesley Morris (2019) describes the ways in which African American musicians changed the musical and cultural landscape as they considered "how to move not only music forward, but American culture forward" (Morris, 2019). They reimagined instrumental sounds outside of "Western European classical music … taking music to a place that nobody had ever tried to previously take it" (Morris, 2019). By expanding the epistemic boundaries of our music classrooms, we make space for our students to experience the multifaceted ways in which music can sound, function, and represent the rich musical diversity of our world.

The epistemic expansion of our music teaching, as Paris and Alim (2017) and Domínguez (2017) remind us, provides students with access to multiple music traditions but it also provides a space in which students' own musical-cultural identities can be sustained. We sustain the musical cultures of our students by celebrating their musical diversity, by emphasizing the musical histories and traditions that provide meaning and empowerment for those marginalized by society and have oftentimes been erased in mainstream education. Love (2019), in her discussion about abolitionist teaching and educational freedom, asserts that "what we who are dark want is to matter" (p. 15).

Mattering requires visibility, recognition, and the celebration of that which is foundational for our students' identities. For our students to feel recognized and celebrated, their musical ways of being must be fully present within the frameworks of our music teaching. Love (2019) describes this presence as a celebration of students'

> entire selves, past, present, and future. Their ancestors, their family members, their friends, their religion, their music, their dress, their language, the ways they express their gender and sexuality, and their communities must all be embraced and loved. Schools must support the fullness of dark life as a way to justice.
>
> (pp. 120–121)

In our music classrooms, are we supporting the fullness of our students' lives? Do we provide opportunities for our students to be fully themselves? Or, are our classrooms spaces in which students feel inhibited, misunderstood, or worse, punished and disciplined because of who they are?

For students to "matter" in our music classrooms, we must not only recognize and celebrate their musical cultures, but we are implored to teach about the ways in which our students' musical cultures are part of our collective musical history. In the third episode of the *New York Times'* audio series "1619," from the "1619 Project" entitled "The Birth of American Music," Wesley Morris (2019) illuminates the ways in which Black music has influenced American musical culture; in fact, he asserts, "Black music is American music," it is the "sound of America." That sound, according to Morris, is the sound of "possibility [and] struggle"—the "sound of a people who, for decades and centuries, have been denied freedom." It is because of that struggle that, in Morris' words,

> Black music is the ultimate expression of a belief in that freedom, the belief that the struggle is worth it, that the pain begets joy, and that that joy you're experiencing is not only contagious, it's necessary and urgent and irresistible. Black music is American music.
>
> (Morris, 2019)

In our music classrooms, do we celebrate our students' musical cultures? Do we celebrate the contributions and influence of their musical cultures? Or do we designate one month a year to discuss their musical histories, highlighting only the strife and not the power? African American music has empowered, influenced, emboldened, inspired, and changed American musical life. Do we communicate this history to our students? Do we communicate to our students that we know the power, history, hope, beauty, and struggle of their musical cultures? When we communicate to our students that we know the complexities, history, and the vast influence of their music, we are communicating to them that we *see* them. That they matter. For us to be able to see our students, however, we must *know* our students and their musical histories. This requires an expansion of our own epistemologies. Because, as Love (2019) reminds us,

> The idea that dark people have had no impact on history or the progress of mankind is one of the foundational ideas of White supremacy. Denying dark people's existence and contributions to human progress relegates dark folx to being takers and not cocreators of history or their lives.
>
> (Love, 2019, p. 14)

To celebrate our students' musical cultures is to understand them, deeply, to recognize their worth, their power, and the ways in which they have contributed to our collective musical history.

## 148 *Moving Forward*

By recognizing their musical histories, we can better understand how their musical cultures are impactful in the present. Epistemic expansion allows us to make that which has been invisible—visible. Music and the arts provide a means by which to connect home and school. Love reminds us that schools, for most BIPOC, are hostile environments and places of "dark suffering" (Love, 2019, p. 15). Music classrooms, therefore, can be places in which students find their cultural centeredness within this hostile environment and the courage to persist in the face of hostility.

> Art education in schools is so important because, for many dark children, art is more than classes or a mode of expression; it is how dark children make sense of this unjust world and a way to sustain who they are, as they recall and (re)member in the mist of chaos what it means to thrive. For many dark folx, art is a homeplace; art is where they find a voice that feels authentic and rooted in participatory democracy.
>
> (Love, 2019, p. 100)

How can our music classrooms be a "homeplace" for all that enter? How might we expand our boundaries to recognize and empower those who have traditionally been forgotten? Love (2019) so eloquently describes the arts as "freedom dreams" (p. 100). Do the methods, assumptions, and traditions on which music education is based provide space for "freedom dreams?" Do our music teaching practices embolden our students towards the kind of musical inspiration, sustenance, remembering, and dreaming that Love describes? If not, it is time that they do so. It is long overdue.

## References

Brown v. Board of Education, 347 U.S. 483 (1954).

Domínguez, M. (2017). "Se hace puentes al andar:" Decolonial teacher education as a needed bridge to culturally sustaining and revitalizing pedagogies. In D. Paris & H. S. Alim (Eds.), *Culturally sustaining pedagogies: Teaching and learning for justice in a changing world* (pp. 225–245). Teachers College Press.

Fairclough, A. (2004). The costs of Brown: Black teachers and school integration. *The Journal of American History*, 91(1), 43–55. doi:10.2307/3659612.

Love, B. L. (2019). *We want to do more than survive: Abolitionist teaching and the pursuit of educational freedom*. Beacon Press.

Morris, J. E. (2008). Research, ideology, and the Brown decision: Counter-narratives to the historical and contemporary representation of Black schooling. *Teachers College Record*, 110(4), 713–732.

Morris, W. (2019, September 6). The birth of American music. *New York Times*, 1619, episode 3. https://www.nytimes.com/2019/09/06/podcasts/1619-black-america n-music-appropriation.html.

My Music Class[TM]. *National Association for Music Education*. https://nafme.org/m y-music-class/.

Paris, D. (2012). Culturally sustaining pedagogy: A needed change in stance, terminology, and practice. *Educational Researcher*, 41(3), 93–97. doi:10.3102/0013189x12441244.

Paris, D., & Alim, H. S. (Eds.). (2017). *Culturally sustaining pedagogies: Teaching and learning for justice in a changing world*. Teachers College Press.

Robinson-Martin, T. (2017). *So you want to sing gospel: A guide for performers*. Rowman & Littlefield.

Trei, L. (2004, 21 April). Black children might have been better off without *Brown v. Board*, Bell says. *Stanford Report*. https://news.stanford.edu/news/2004/april21/brownbell-421.html.

# Index

abolitionist teaching 3
Abril, C. 11, 13
ABRSM Music Certification System 35–36
ABRSM systems 61
academic success 5
achievement gap 15–16
active music-making 94–95
aesthetics 10, 32, 34–36, 61, 63–64, 66–67, 113
African American music: gospel singing 143; jazz tradition 138; musicians 146; rap 92; schools 144–145; students 5; worship style 45; *see also* Black music
African American Vernacular English (AAVE) 91
African music: drumming 14; elements of 92
Afrocentric teaching 145–146
Alim, H. S. 7–8, 12, 146
Allsup, R. E. 110
*American Annals of Education and Instruction* 53
American Indians, miseducation 38
Americanization 67
American Missionary Association (AMA) 45
American music education 28, 147
anatomical physicality 113
appreciation of music 66
appropriateness 8; discourses of 16, 116; racist discourses of 109; and superiority 109
Arabic music: folk song 14; *mawaal* 143
assimilationism 16, 67
assumptions 141
aural transmission 146
autonomy 94

*Baltimore Sun* 44
Beethoven sonata 14
*bel canto* singing technique 58, 60, 67, 112–113
belief systems 4–5; about music and singing 107; listening and singing 66; and practices 141–142
Bell, D. 144
Benedict, C. 110–111
Bethel African Methodist Episcopal (AME) Church 46
betterment: auspices 32; discourses 27, 35; moral 54–55; social 30
Birge, E. 64
Black, Indigenous, People of Color (BIPOC) 79
Black children, culture of 145
Black music 114, 147; *see also* African American music
body: entrainment and vocal expression 118–119; movement 138; percussion 14, 87–88, 112, 137–138
Boston Academy of Music 55, 58
Brahms symphony 14
Brazilian *Embolada* 92–93
breath management for singing 33
British musical colonialism 28
Britton, A. 27–29
*Brown v. Board of Education* 144–145
Brubeck, D. 137
Bucholtz, M. 7, 117
Burlin, N. C. 136

Calderon, D. 26
Carlisle Indian Boarding School 39–45; *Baltimore Sun* 44; classical vocal teaching 42; cultural genocide 43; curriculum 42; government-funded 39; Indian problem 43; musical

## Index 151

qualities 42; racialized musical hegemony 42–43; savages 40; trauma 41–42; *Washington Evening Star* 45; Western classical musical teaching 44

character improvement and music education: Mason and Pestalozzi 55–57; Mason's influence and moral imperative 57–58; musical tastes 54; sound judgement 54; Woodbridge and Fellenberg 53–54

Chicanx communities 13

children: of color, cultures of 5; cultural identities 5; learning 57; musical cultures 16–17

choralism 29

choral performance 56

Christianity 27–28

Christian saviorism 38

Civilization Fund Act 38

civilizing 27, 38, 72

classical piano music 137

classical vocal technique 33, 42

classroom: communication style and behavior 144–145; discipline 107; K-12 116; management 95, 116–117; student and teacher, alienation in 110; *see also* music classrooms

Coates, T. N. 26

codification of music education standards 68

colonialism/colonialist 108; beliefs 111; discourses 108, 111; history 16; racist music teaching practices 27; thinking 28

coloniality 8, 107–109

communication style, and classroom behavior 144–145

composer and score 136

Congolese singing 143

contemporary music teaching discourses 25

convert, music education 27

creative liberation 14

critical race theory 118

critical raciolinguistic perspective 7

Croatian Bećarac 143

culture/cultural 65; competence 5; equity 109; genocide 27, 43; identity 5; incongruence 90–91; orientation 117; plurality 6, 8, 15; relevance 107; responsiveness 13; skills 14; sustenance 7; synchronization 117

culturally sustaining pedagogy (CSP) 20, 140; aims 6; analysis 14; cultural

plurality 15; cultural practices within 7–8; dismantle raciolingustic ideologies 17; educators challenge 13; as framework 14; for music education 10–20; and open musical epistemology 116–118

curriculum: Carlisle Indian Boarding School 42; musical repertoire and 107; non-traditional music teaching approaches 93–95; and pedagogy 112–113; pre-programmed and lesson plans 111

Curwen, J. 30–31, 33–34, 56, 60

Damrosch, W. 61–62

decolonial teacher education 110

decolonization 109, 118–119

default theory 5

DiAngelo, R. 3

discipline 27, 86–87, 95

disciplining choralism 28

diverse musical epistemologies 14

diversity 4, 74

Dominant American English 16–17

dominant knowledge systems 16

Domínguez, M. 7, 110, 120, 146

Drury, R. 30–31

Dunbar-Ortiz, R. 26

education/educational: climate 5; discourse 66; equity 7; freedom 3; inequality 108–109; justice 6; reform movements 15; scholarship 5; success 12; theories 4–5

educators 141

Eidsheim, N. S. 17–18

elitism 142

encouragement, over discipline 101–102

epistemic travel 119–121

epistemology 107

equity 74

ethical crisis 110

ethnicity 18

eugenics 70

Eurocentricity/Eurocentric 73; epistemology 142–143; musical epistemology 10, 20, 73, 107, 111; *see also* non-Eurocentric music traditions

Euro-elitism 28

European music, in America 27

exclusion 73

extroverted body accentuation 113

## 152 Index

fear of singing 88–89
Fellenberg, P. E. von 53–54
Fisk Jubilee Singers 45–50, 135–136; audiences' perceptions and reaction 48–50; discipline 46–48; musical culture 48; musical embodiment and musical entrainment 48; singers' performance 48; Tonic Sol-Fa movement 47; vocal ideology 47; vocal tone 47; Western classical vocal pedagogy 46
fixed-doh sight-singing approach 28
Flores, N. 7, 16–17, 116
forced labor 39
freedom dreams 148
French Jesuits, and music 27
funds of knowledge 7, 15

Gante, Pedro de 27
Garcia, M. 33
Gay, G. 6, 10, 116–117
genocide 26–27, 30, 43
gestures 111, 113
Glenn, M. 64
globalization 4
global pandemic 4
Gould, E. 120
grade process 36
Grubb, W. N. 4
Gustafson, R. I. 109, 113, 115

*Hampton Series Negro Folk-Songs* 136
head voice 113–114
heathen, music education 27
hegemony/hegemonic 27; Eurocentric discourses, dismantling 118–119; system of power 62
heritage musical practices 15
hip hop 14, 143–144
Holt, H. E. 61
Hullah, F. 28
Hungarian society 70

identity 80–82
ignorance 15
imagination 14
immigrant population 4
immigration 65
improvisation 137
inclusivity 69
Indian Removal Act of 1830 38
Indigenouscentric teaching 145–146; *see also* Native Americans

Indigenous musical traditions 27; *see also* Native Americans
inequality 3–4, 25, 74, 108–109
infantilization 70
inhibited singers 114
institutional racism 73
intergenerational cultural practices 7, 20
internal colonialism 28
*Itinerant Curriculum Theory* 118
Ives, E. 55

Jaramillo, N. 15
jazz 137–138
Jesuits 27
*Juvenile Lyre* 55
K-12 education: classrooms 11, 116; music classrooms 108; music 58; music teaching 68; schools 109; student demographics 17; teachers 6
Kaffirs 31–32
Keene, J. A. 57
Kodály, Z. 70

Ladson-Billings, G. 5
language agency 7
Latinx-centric teaching 145–146
*Laurel Music-Reader* publication, 1919 63
Laurel Series of songs 63
Lee, J. S. 7
Leonardo, Z. 4
Lind, V. R. 11
linguistics: and cultural competence 8; diversity 4; hierarchy 7; plurality and educational settings 7; purity 7, 16
listening and whiteness 16–19
literacy 14
Love, B. L. 26, 136, 142, 144, 146–148

Malaysian *Dondang Sayang* 143
Maldonado-Torres, N. 108
Malewski, E. 15
mannerisms 65
manual labor schools 39
*Manual of the Boston Academy of Music: For Instruction in the Elements of Vocal Music, on the System of Pestalozzi* 55, 57
*Mariachi* singing 143
Mason, L. 47, 54, 60, 67–68
mass migration 4
McConathy, O. 64
McKoy, C. L. 11
melting pot 68–69

## Index   153

Merriam, S. B. 113
Mexican heritage 13
middle-class linguistic 14
Miessner, O. 64
minoritized communities,
    intergenerational cultural practices 20
mono-musical educational paradigm 14–15
Monroe, C. R. 117
moral development 54
morality 64
Morris, J. E. 144–145
Morris, W. 146–147
Morrison, T. 12
MSNC standards 68
Mulligan, G. 137
multicultural education 6, 13
multiculturalism 68–69, 72
music/musical: appreciation 67, 146; and
    civilizing mission 27–28; colonialism
    27; communities, marginalized 120;
    compositions 66; conquest 27–28;
    consumers 141; cultures 13–14, 146;
    curriculum and pedagogy 112–113;
    diversity 72; education, culturally
    responsive 10–11; and educational
    saviorism 16; educators 14, 33, 72, 74,
    116; epistemology 117; exclusions
    116; expressivity 146; and family
    82–84; feeling 57; genocide 30;
    hierarchy, perpetuation 73; ignorance,
    of society 70; justice 15; listening 146;
    literacy 13, 134, 135, 146; moralism
    28; movements 61; performance 146;
    preservation 73; proficiency 57;
    repertoire and curriculum 107;
    saviorism 12, 27, 72; standards 146;
    story-telling 146; taste 66
music epistemology and music
    education: classroom management,
    paradox of 116–117; closed musical
    epistemology 107–116; coloniality
    107–109; culturally sustaining
    pedagogy 116–118; culture sustains
    117–118; discourses of appropriate-
    ness 116; epistemic travel 119–121;
    Eurocentric framework 118–119;
    open 116–118
music classrooms 148; cultural plurality
    99–100; encouragement over discipline
    101–102; opportunity to express
    themselves 101; singing 102–103;
    students value autonomy 100–101
music education 53; and assimilationism
    68–69; CSP for 10–20; education,

dismantling 140–143; embracing
    145–148; epistemologies of ignorance
    15–16; epistemology 35–36;
    expanding 143–145; leaders 65;
    listening and whiteness 16–19; new
    mainstream 13–15; ontological
    distance and paradigm 19–20;
    practice 36; standardization and
    codification 60–74; White gaze,
    refusing 12–13
*Music Education Source Books* 69
Music Educators National Conference
    (MENC) 28, 69
musicians 141
*Music in American Education* 71
music-making techniques 69–70
music pedagogy, culturally sustaining
    12–13, 20, 25, 144
Music Supervisors National Conference
    (MSNC) 65
music teaching approaches 69, 71;
    culturally responsive 13; culturally
    sustaining 97; disrupts 120; methods
    25; non-traditional 91–97; practices
    and ideology 141; traditional 86–91
music teaching practices, normalized:
    Black, Indigenous, People of Color
    (BIPOC) 79; constant comparative
    method of analysis 80; data-analysis
    spiral 80; data collection methods
    80; music and family 82–84;
    self-expression and identity 80–82
My Music Class[TM] 140

Nabokov, P. 40
Nägeli, H. G. 53, 57
National Association for Music
    Education (NAfME) 65, 69, 73,
    133, 140
nationalism 13
*National Music Course* 60
National Society for Study of Education 28
National Supervisor's Conference 66
Native Americans: children 39;
    educational colonization 38; family
    and social dysfunction 39–40;
    testimony 40–41; *see also*
    Indigenouscentric teaching;
    Indigenous musical traditions
neo-colonialist discourses 109
non-Eurocentric music traditions 135
non-singer 64
non-traditional music teaching approaches
    91–97; culturally sustaining music

## 154 *Index*

teaching 97; curriculum 93–95; student agency and musical autonomy 91–92; vocal empowerment 96–97; vocal teaching, description of 95–96; *see also* traditional music teaching approaches
non-Western epistemologies 26
nuances 107, 114

Obidah, J. E. 117
objective racialization 111
Ogden, J. 45
Olwage, G. 29
ontological distance 91, 110–111
Orff, C. 69
Orff music teaching method 70, 91, 112
ostinati 70

Paraskeva, J. M. 119–120
Paris, D. 4–5, 8, 12, 14, 146
Parker, H. 64–65
Patel, L. 109
pedagogy/pedagogical 66; bridges 10; culturally relevant and responsive 4–6; culturally responsive 10–11; epistemology 14; nuance 107
pentatonic scale 70
performance practices 10
performers 141
Perkins, W. O. 31–32
personal entrainment 112
Pestalozzi, J. H. 53
Pestalozzian philosophy 60
Pfeiffer, M. T. 53
physical harm 41
pitch variance 113
pluralistic society 6
political domination 7
popular music 63
posture and body containment 88
practical implications: beliefs and assumptions 127–129; Choral Pre-High School Unit 134–137; critical inquiry and current practices analysis 127–133; inquiry and interrogation 129–130; kindergarten "General Music Responding Unit" 137–138; multi-epistemic approach 130–133; responding units 133–134
Pratt, R. H. 39
pre-programmed curriculum and lesson plans 111
pre-service education programs 6
*Progressive Music Series* 64–65
psychological and cultural brainwashing 41

Quantz, R. 114, 117
quartet 137
queer theory 118
quo music teaching assumptions 27

race/racial: of entrainment 111; historical ideology 114; incitements 109; inequality 4; musical hegemony 42–43; or language-minoritized communities 17; and racism, music education 107; remedies 118
raciomusical ideologies 17
racism 26, 107
racist structures 13
*Red Man, The* 42
refinement 27
reformer 28
resource pedagogies 5
rhythmic or musical patterns 70
Ripley, F. H. 60–61
ritual 107
Robinson-Martin, T. M. 113
Rosa, J. 7, 16–17, 116
Ross, C. 73

*Samba* dance steps 93
savage, music education 27
saviorism 27, 142
saxophones 137
Schenkerian analysis 14
scholarship, fluidity of 6
schools and educational spaces 142–143
second-generation individuals 4
Seiler, E. 34
self-concept 4
self-consciousness 35
self-expression 14, 80–82, 94
Sensoy, O. 3
settler colonialism 26
Seward, T. F. 32, 46, 56, 136
Shaw, J. T. 10
Simon, E. 44
singers: caste of 56; classification system 64; inhibited 114; non- 64; performance 48; silenced 113
singing 102–103; bodies 118–119; conception of correct 62–63; cultured style of 113–114; and musical cultivation 56; posture 33; technique 56; tone 33; *see also specific types/ techniques*
slavery 39
Sleeter, C. E. 13
Social Darwinism and discourses 69, 70

## Index    155

social justice 3, 108
socio-political consciousness 5
sound, appraisal of 18–19
Spanish Franciscan Catholic missions 27
Spanish language 16
Spell, L. 27
spirituality 72
Spradley, M. V 74
standardization and codification, music
 education: adolescent voice teaching
 63–64; bureaucratization 65–74;
 methods and philosophy 69–71;
 musical saviorism and universalism
 61–63; musical taste and music
 appreciation 64–65; music courses
 and vocal pedagogy 60–61; music
 supervisors national conference and
 standards 65–69; National
 Association of Music Education and
 Equity 72–74; western classical
 musical superiority 71–72
Stoever, J. L. 17
students: agency 91–92, 103; behavior
 86–87; of color, linguistic and cultural
 heritage 7; cultural competencies 5,
 13; cultural identities 8, 10; cultural
 practices 121; expressions, linguistic
 and colloquial 117; interest 86–87;
 linguistic practices 116; misbehavior
 86–87; musical-cultural identities 10;
 musical epistemologies 97; musical
 exploration 92; and teacher,
 alienation in classroom 110; value
 autonomy 100–101; value cultural
 plurality 99–100; value opportunity
 to express themselves 101; vocal
 confidence 97
superiority 108

Tanglewood symposium 73
Tapper, T. 60–61
teacher education 5, 7
teaching, culturally responsive 6
theory 3
Tomlins, W. 63
Tonic Sol-Fa approach 29–30, 38, 61;
 ABRSM Music Certification
 System, precursor for 35–36; music
 certification system 30; music teachers
 30; Western Classical Vocal Pedagogy
 33–35
traditional music teaching approaches
 86–91; disciplining and silencing of
 bodies and voices 86–88; implications

90–91; strict vocal approach—Western
 classical style 88–89; vocal inhibition
 89–90; *see also* non-traditional music
 teaching approaches
*Traveller, The* 48
Tufts, J. W. 61

uncivilized subject, music education as 27
United States, civilizing mission in:
 Carlisle Indian Boarding School
 40–45; Fisk Jubilee Singers 45–50
*Universal Music Series* 62, 65
unvoiced speech 114–115
utility of choralism 29

verbal and nonverbal communication
 patterns 79
Victorian choralism movement 28
Vietnamese *Ca trù* singing 143
*Vision 2020: The Housewright
 Symposium on the Future of Music
 Education* 72
vocal-cultural identities 67
vocality 128, 130–131
vocals/vocal: aesthetics 63–64; confidence
 97; discipline 34; empowerment 96–97;
 habits 67; hegemony in music
 education 67–68; pedagogy 33–34, 57;
 production 64; quality 35; teaching
 methods 33, 60–61, 63, 67, 95–96;
 technique 56, 61; traditions 143
vocational training 13
voice, quality of 34–35, 60

*Washington Evening Star* 45
Watson, J. 46
we got talent (WGT) 96
Westerlund, H. 110
Western classical music/musical 10, 27,
 66; aesthetics 63, 71; canon 73;
 education 61, 91; epistemology
 135; European 146; hegemony 25;
 hierarchy 14; knowledge system 13;
 notation 146; paradigm 13; pedagogy
 and ranking system 30; practices 70;
 primitive 26; savage 26; singing 48;
 standards 16; teaching 36, 44;
 terminology 138; tradition 142;
 training 42; vocal pedagogy 33–35,
 91; vocal production, aesthetics of 64;
 vocal technique 56
Western music colonialism 27
White gaze 12, 19
White listening ear 19

## 156   Index

White mainstream society 4–5
whiteness and racism 17
White privileged classical musician 136
White supremacy 39, 147
White teachers 17; *see also* non-Western
 epistemologies

Woodbridge, W. C. 53–54
woodwind instruments 137
*World of Music* series 64
Wright, D. C. 35

Zulus 31–32

Printed in the United States
by Baker & Taylor Publisher Services